KIDZ BOP BE A POP STAR!

Start Your Own Band, Book Your Own Gigs, and Become a ROCK PHENOM!

Kimberly Potts

Aadamsmedia
Avon, Massachusetts

Copyright © 2011 by F+W Media, Inc.
All rights reserved.
This book, or parts thereof, may not be reproduced in any
form without permission from the publisher; exceptions are
made for brief excerpts used in published reviews.

Published by
Adams Media, a division of F+W Media, Inc.
57 Littlefield Street, Avon, MA 02322. U.S.A.
www.adamsmedia.com

ISBN 10: 1-4405-0572-1
ISBN 13: 978-1-4405-0572-0
eISBN 10: 1-4405-0894-1
eISBN 13: 978-1-4405-0894-3

Printed by RR Donnelley, Harrisonburg, VA, US

10   9   8   7   6   5   4   3   2   1

June 2011

Library of Congress Cataloging-in-Publication Data
is available from the publisher.

Man with Guitar Illustration on page 1 © Neubau Welt
Girl with Guitar Illustration on page 43 © istockphoto AskinTulayOver
Man with Guitar Illustration on page 123 © istockphoto 4x6
Girl Jumping Illustration on page 167 © istockphoto AskinTulayOver

This book is available at quantity discounts for bulk purchases.
For information, please call 1-800-289-0963.

PART ONE

Eva Elijah Steffan Hanna Charisma

CHAPTER 1
A KIDZ BOP Pop Star Is Born

So you say you wanna be a pop star. Okay, but seriously, you should know that life as you now know it? Soooo over. And that's a good thing.

Not that there's anything wrong with your life as it is now. And not that being a pop star is for everyone (check out our checklists below to see if you were born to be one). But if you have your heart—and, just as important, your mind and your commitment to hard work—set on becoming a pop star, the fact is that you probably aren't going to be satisfied until you make it happen. And making it happen, the process of making it happen, and the life you'll live once pop stardom is a thing of your future, means you most definitely will have to bid adieu to your old lifestyle . . .

All-night weekend sleepovers and Twilight movie marathons with your BFFs? Sure . . . but only if it doesn't prevent you from getting the sleep you need to make sure you're fresh, fine, and ready to deliver a spectacular performance at that audition tomorrow morning.

Heading off to Applebee's for afterschool snacks and a major gossip catch-up with the crew? Sometimes . . . but only on the days you're not meeting with your vocal coach, going to a dance class, or scoping out potential bass players for your all-grrrl rock band.

Catching the latest Rob Pattinson flick at the mall? Well, okay, some things don't change. Besides, it's research for when you launch your Justin Timberlake–ish triple-threat career as a singer/dancer/actor, right?

The point is, pursuing your pop stardom goals means sacrificing some of the time you usually spend on other pursuits. Of course, it also means doing what you're passionate about, sharing your creative talents with audiences, meeting new people and seeing new places, experiencing fame, and, yes, in the case of some pop superstars, fortune.

It means living your dreams.

So, what are you waiting for? Farewell, old life . . . and hellooooo, stardom!

KIDZ BOP KIDS ON: STARDOM

Who knows more about what it takes to be a pop star than the KIDZ BOP Kids? No one! That's why, throughout the book, we'll get the scoop straight from the pop stars'—or in this case, the BOP stars'—mouths! Here's Steffan, Hanna, Eva, Elijah, and Charisma with their top tips on living the pop star life:

STEFFAN: "Eat right, work out every day, and get as much sleep as you can. Now I know why my mom is always bugging me to eat more fruit and veggies, less candy and pizza. Being a pop star is fun, but it's also *work*! I get a workout every time I'm onstage, and the better I feel, the more sleep I can get, the better I can perform."

HANNA: "I listen to music any time I'm not singing, and I listen to all kinds of music, not just the stuff I like. I'm always asking friends and family members what their favorite music is, and then I check it out. My English teacher told us that one of the best ways to become a good writer is to read a lot, because it helps you get a feel for words and the way they're used. I think the same thing is true for singers. Listening to other singers, and the way they phrase things and their tones, just makes me a better singer. And listening to different kinds of music is helping me find my own vocal style."

EVA: "When I got a new cell phone for my birthday, I asked for one that has a built-in voice recorder. It's with me at all times—okay, all times except when I'm showering—and when a lyric, or the way I want to sing a certain verse or a certain note, or even an idea for a stage outfit pops into my head, I record myself singing or I make myself a 'voice note' about it."

ELIJAH: "I do the same thing that Eva does, except that I use a little notebook that I carry with me everywhere (okay, no, also not into the shower). Eva always teases me that I could just speak into my phone or take notes on my phone, but I just like the feeling of writing down all my thoughts, ideas, notes, etc., with a pen and paper. It feels more creative to me. Plus, I like to sketch ideas for stage designs, outfits, and flyers to promote KIDZ BOP Kids. In my notebook, I even have a sketch of the exact outfit I'm going to wear when I win my first MTV VMA statue, and the killer suit I'm going to wear when I win my first Grammy."

CHARISMA: "What Elijah said about winning an MTV award and a Grammy . . . that's the biggest thing, I think, is just to believe and constantly remind yourself that those things are possible. When you dream of being a pop star, or an actress, or a dancer, or whatever your star dream is, it can seem overwhelming and impossible to achieve. But it isn't . . . we're all proof of that! There are always opportunities to show your talent, like in the KIDZ Star USA Talent Search, and local talent shows and TV shows like *American Idol* and *America's Got Talent*. And sometimes you have to make your own opportunities, like making YouTube clips of your performances, or making your own webshow for KIDZBOP.com. It's just important, if you're really passionate about being a pop star, to always be thinking about how you can make that happen, always be working toward making it happen, and most of all, to believe that it can really happen."

Nine Signs You Were Born to Be a Pop Star . . .

1. You love to sing, anywhere, anytime, in the shower, on the way to school . . . even while doing the dishes after dinner!
2. Singing, and performing, doesn't seem like hard work to you . . . it's your passion.
3. You know you're talented . . . but you also know you can be even better. And you want to be the best!
4. You can't wait to start working with a vocal coach, a stylist, songwriters, record company executives, publicists . . . all the people on Team Make-You-a-Star.
5. You like to record yourself singing your favorite songs.
6. You love to sing so much that you would do it for free (and, in the beginning, sometimes will!).
7. Time with your friends and family is important, but you're willing to make sacrifices to achieve your pop star dreams.
8. You can't wait to be famous, having your photo taken all the time, your name in magazines and on gossip websites, getting to wear fabulous clothes and meeting your fellow celebs!
9. You simply wouldn't be happy if you didn't put your time, energy, efforts, and talents into pursuing your pop star dreams.

And Nine Signs You Were Not

1. You like to sing . . . but not in front of other people.
2. There are lots of things you enjoy doing, some of them much more than you enjoy singing.
3. Singing is your hobby, but you can't imagine it being your job.
4. The idea of practicing, working with a vocal coach, singing the same songs over and over and over and . . . well, it sounds more like homework than something fun.

5. You like to record yourself making obnoxious noises.

6. Free?! You don't even do chores for free . . . that's why your parents give you an allowance!

7. There is only one time in your life to truly be a teenager, so friends, fam, and fun first! You have plenty of time after college to make your career dreams come true . . . once you figure out what those dreams are.

8. You think meeting your favorite stars would be cool, but who wants to have to be photo-ready all the time? Besides, sometimes those magazines and gossip shows can be mean! You don't want to end up getting dissed on TMZ!

9. You simply wouldn't be happy putting your time, energy, efforts, and talents into pursuing pop stardom.

Are You Ready to Rock Like a KIDZ BOP Kid?

Pardon the cliché, but it's completely true in this instance: Being a pop star isn't all fun and games. It is fun, of course . . . lots of fun. But it's also a lot of hard work, and a lot of time away from other things you like to do, and away from people you want to spend time with. It's also totally worth it to achieve your pop stardom dreams, to have fun, travel the world, see new places, and meet new people you might not otherwise have the chance to see and meet, but before jumping in with both feet, it's really important to think about how much time and effort you're willing to commit to your budding music career.

Do you want to be an international star, à la Lady Gaga or Justin Bieber? Would you be happy being an American star? Or maybe keeping your talent local is more your thang, playing school functions and social events around town? All three levels of musical career require skills, practice, time, and endless hours of devotion to reaching your goals, so again, the question comes down to: Are you ready to rock like a KIDZ BOP pop star?

Maybe this will help you decide. Here's a look at a day in the life of the average international pop star. You'll note it's quite a packed schedule, and it's important to note that once you actually achieve a certain level of success, whatever level that is, the hard work only continues . . .

A Day in the Life of a KIDZ BOP Kid

★ **6 A.M.**—Rise and shine! If you don't have media interviews scheduled this early (and sometimes you will; remember, being a global superstar means you have to be available to do interviews in various time zones), it just means you have the chance to eat a healthy breakfast and get in some energy-boosting exercise at the gym!

★ **7 A.M.**—Go over your schedule for the day. Then, at 7:10, officially begin the work day with a round of morning radio interviews.

★ **8 A.M.**— You head off to the *Seventeen* magazine offices in New York City for an interview. Good thing you like talking about yourself, right? And as soon as you finish at *Seventeen*, start warming up your singing pipes, because you're on your way to the studios of *Live with Regis & Kelly*, where you'll be performing your new (soon to be a number-one hit!) song.

★ **9 A.M.**—A meeting with your stylist to finalize a wardrobe for your tour.

★ **10 A.M.**—Grab a Sharpie or five . . . it's time to sign photos, CD booklets, posters, and other promotional materials that are going to be distributed to your fans. PS—Hope you have a steady hand, because you're signing all these autographs while in a van, surrounded by your publicist, manager, a record company executive and at least two of their assistants, on your way to another appearance: *The View*.

★ **11 A.M.**—You arrive at *The View*, and continue signing autographs while waiting for your on-screen time, during which you will again perform your new song, and chat with the hosts about everyone's favorite topic: you!

★ **Noon—Lunch!** Which you'll eat on the way to a meeting with a major movie studio, whose executives want to talk to you and your people about filming a concert movie, starring you, in 3-D!

★ **1 P.M.—School!** You may be a pop star, but that doesn't mean you can get away without getting an education! You have to spend at least three hours a day with your tutor studying—it's the law! So hit the books and learn something, already!

★ **4 P.M.**—Vocal workout with your singing coach (yes, even successful musicians continue to work with vocal coaches).

★ **5 P.M.**—Head to a downtown NYC studio for a photo shoot for your next CD.

★ **6 P.M.**—Photo shoot.

★ **7 P.M.**—Dinner! Which you'll scarf down on the way back to your hotel, after the photo shoot.

★ **8 P.M.**—Homework. You're getting off easy tonight, with just a couple of pages of math problems to do.

★ **9 P.M.**—You want to wind down for the night, but you're too excited about a specific meeting you have lined up for tomorrow, the one in which you'll discuss how you're going to launch your own iPhone app.

★ **9:30 P.M.**—Finally! It's time to go to bed, and after your long day, you're ready to fall asleep as soon as your head hits the pillow. Or, after you scribble some notes for that song idea that just popped into your head . . .

★ **10 P.M.**—You fall asleep. So you can get up and have another crazy, amazing day.

PS—Imagine this particular day in the life of a pop star again—only this time in summer. Sure, you wouldn't have to work with your tutor or homework—but you'd be just as busy, off on location shooting your first feature film!

So, still think you're ready to embark on the pop star life? Try this:

Pop Quiz: Are You Ready to Rock?

Before you embark on this thing called pop stardom, try this little quiz to make sure it's truly something you're interested in . . .

1. **Your favorite way to spend a Saturday afternoon is . . .**
   A. Watching a marathon of *iCarly* on Nickelodeon
   B. Hanging at the mall with your friends
   C. Loading up your iPod with new tunes
   D. Reading a great book

2. **Your fashion style can best be described as . . .**
   A. Fabulous
   B. Trendy
   C. Funky
   D. Comfortable

3. **The best thing about being a pop star would be . . .**
   A. Signing autographs
   B. Everyone knows who you are
   C. Getting paid to do something you love
   D. Not having to have a "real job"

4. **It's Monday afternoon, and you get an assignment to write a five-page research paper on your favorite band, due Friday afternoon! When do you start working on the report?**
   A. Thursday evening
   B. Friday morning
   C. Monday evening
   D. Wednesday afternoon

5. **Finish this sentence: Hard work is . . .**
   A. . . . unnecessary; I work smart, not hard.
   B. . . . for other people.

C. . . . necessary to achieve big things.

D. . . . not worth it.

Grading your score on the quiz is simple: If you truly are ready to rock like a pop star, most, if not all, of your answers should have been "**C.**" If you chose mostly As, Bs, or Ds, well, this whole pop star thang might not be what you really want.

Pop Star Mashup: Breakdown of a KIDZ BOP Kid

A KIDZ BOP pop star is many things. Does this mashup of pop star-ness sound like you?

A KIDZ BOP pop star . . .

★ is a music lover.

★ is passionate about his or her interests.

. . . loves to try new things.

★ loves to meet new people.

★ knows that hard work brings big rewards.

★ knows you must work hard to achieve your goals.

★ dreams of performing music for an appreciative crowd.

★ but is also happy playing air guitar and rocking out in front of his or her mirror.

★ dreams big.

★ is willing to practice to become a skilled singer/musician/song-writer/dancer/performer.

★ understands that even when he or she achieves success, practice and hard work will be necessary to maintain and improve upon that success.

★ is willing to seek out help and advice from other musicians, especially those who've *unsuccessfully* pursued a career in the music industry.

★ is willing to seek out help and advice from other musicians, especially those who've unsuccessfully pursued a career in the music industry (they may have a different, equally valuable perspective on the matter).

★ is also willing to learn about the business side of pursuing a music career. Talent is tops, but thousands of really talented musicians have failed to achieve their musical dreams because they didn't bother to learn about the business of being a musician.

★ is confident. If you don't believe you can become a pop star, no one else will either.

★ is motivated. If you're not willing to do everything you can to realize your dreams, no one else is going to be motivated to help you achieve them, either.

★ makes a grand plan. Imagine what achieving your ultimate goal would look like, then make a list of the steps you'll have to take to make it happen. Don't know exactly what all those steps are? See "is willing to seek out help and advice from other musicians" above.

★ goes to concerts, talks with other music lovers, and watches music awards shows, *American Idol*, MTV, CMT, Fuse, and any other TV shows where he or she can study what makes other musicians successful and fun to watch.

★ has an understanding of the history of pop music. As the saying goes, those who don't understand history are doomed to repeat it, and that works both ways; by having some knowledge of pop stars of the past, you can learn from their mistakes, and also study what they did right.

★ is fun! As you are no doubt beginning to understand, being a pop star involves a lot of hard work, first, to become successful, and then, to maintain that success. So if you're going to devote all that time and effort and sacrifices to it, it better be fun, right?

VIBE VOCAB: WORDS EVERY KIDZ BOP KID SHOULD KNOW (AND USE!)

A CAPPELLA—Singing without any instrumental accompaniment (like on the TV show *The Sing-Off*).

ACOUSTIC—A performance accompanied only by an instrument like a classical guitar, with no electronic instruments, like in the famous MTV series *Unplugged.* Acoustic performances are particularly good for showing off strong vocal skills and for using a unique arrangement on a well-known song.

BAND—A group of performers, as opposed to a solo artist.

BILLBOARD MAGAZINE—The magazine covering the music industry. *Billboard*'s weekly music charts, which track record sales, are one of the most popular measures of how successful a professional band or singer is. The magazine also has a website, Billboard.com, which features the music charts, music industry news and features, plus interviews with music celebrities and industry executives.

BIO—Short for *biography*. It's important to have a bio of you or your band as part of your publicity efforts. The bio should include information on your personal and professional background, plus interesting tidbits about your likes and dislikes, your musical influences, and your personal and professional accomplishments.

BOOKING—Booking a job means you've made a deal to perform at a venue or event.

BOOKING AGENT—If you don't want to handle booking jobs yourself, you can hire a booking agent, whose job it is to get jobs and negotiate any business issues—payment, performance terms, etc.—for you or your band.

BUSKING—Performing on the street or other public places for tips, as in singing and playing your guitar in the subway in New York City and having passersby throw tips into your hat. Lots of famous musicians had experience busking early in their careers, including Paul McCartney, Sting, Arcade Fire, *American Idol* runner-up Crystal Bowersox, Jon Bon Jovi, Justin Bieber, and Jason Mraz.

COUNTRY—As in country music, a genre of music whose superstars of the past and present include Johnny Cash, Patsy Cline, Loretta Lynn, Conway Twitty, Hank Williams, Willie Nelson, Dolly Parton, Charley Pride, Kenny Rogers, Taylor Swift, Tim McGraw, Brad Paisley, Carrie Underwood, Keith Urban, Faith Hill, Rascal Flatts, Kenny Chesney, and Garth Brooks.

DEMO—*Demo* is short for *demonstration*, a recorded example of your performances that can be shared with record companies and venues that are considering booking you for a job. Demos are usually distributed via CD or digital audio file.

DIVA—A respected female singer, originally used to describe a female opera singer, but now used to describe any popular female singer, like Mariah Carey, Madonna, Lady Gaga, Beyoncé, Mary J. Blige, Whitney Houston, Cher, Christina Aguilera, Britney Spears, Jennifer Lopez, and Fergie.

DIY—Stands for "do it yourself," which you may do a lot as you're trying to get your music career started. Booking your own jobs; creating your own press kits; and DIY marketing, production, and styling duties will most likely be part of the plan to launch you or your band on the path to stardom.

DROP—When a CD is released, it's also "dropped." Example: I can't wait to hear John Mayer's new album, which drops in February.

FANBASE—A group of fans who are dedicated to you and your music. As a new artist, growing a fanbase is the key to your success.

FLIER—Fliers are mini-posters you use to advertise you or your band and any upcoming performances you have scheduled. Fliers can be passed out to people in public, or distributed in public places like school, stores, music venues, and restaurants. (Word of advice: Make sure you have permission to distribute your fliers, especially at school!)

GENRE—The type, or style, of music you perform. Examples of music genres: country, rock, hip-hop, R&B, dance, etc. Most artists fit into one genre but also may combine elements of several different genres, and may also cross over into multiple genres, like Kid Rock, who went from hip-hop to rock to country, and Taylor Swift, whose music is country and pop.

GIG—A job, a performance, a booking.

HEAD SHOT—Whether you're a solo artist or a member of a band, you'll need head shots, or publicity photos, to use as part of your efforts to get attention for your act.

HEADLINER—The singer or band that gets top billing at a concert, i.e., the act who is the most popular/successful at the time, is the headliner act. The singers and bands that perform first, i.e., the act/acts that open the show, are known as the opening acts.

HIP-HOP—As in hip-hop music, a genre of music that originated in New York City in the 1970s, is often meshed with elements of rap, and includes superstars of the past and present such as Will Smith, Run DMC, Gnarls Barkley, and the Black Eyed Peas.

LYRICS—The words in a song.

MANAGER—A person who oversees the business aspects of a performer's or band's career. In many cases, especially with younger artists, the manager may be a parent, who's then sometimes referred to as a "momager" or "dadager."

MARKETING—Literally, getting your music to the market; i.e., making people aware of your music and your performances via fliers, social media promotion, ads, word of mouth, etc.

MEET AND GREET—Usually held before or after a performance, a meet and greet is the chance for your fans to come backstage and meet you, get an autograph, and take photos with you. Many music celebs, record labels, and radio stations use meet and greets as a special prize in contests or for VIP concert guests.

OPENING ACT—The singer or band, usually up-and-coming stars, that open for the headlining singer or band.

PER DIEM—An allowance issued to performers to cover the cost of food and personal expenses.

POP—As in pop music, a genre of music that includes the most commercial, popular music, which often includes elements from other genres and is usually aimed at a younger audience. Superstars of the past and present include Elvis Presley, the Beatles, Elton John, Cher, Donny Osmond, the Beach Boys, Billy Joel, Michael Jackson, 'N Sync, Backstreet Boys, Britney Spears, Mariah Carey, Christina Aguilera, Katy Perry, Lady Gaga, and Justin Bieber.

PRESS KIT—A kit (usually contained within a folder) that includes materials to promote you or your band. A press kit should include a press release with information on your latest projects; a bio of you or your band; publicity photos; a CD of your music; maybe a DVD that features a video performance; a question-and-answer (Q+A) with you and/or the band; and copies of any reviews, blog posts, or features that have been written about you. You can also create an EPK—electronic press kit—which would include the same materials, but instead of distributing them on paper, you would send them to members of the media, potential booking reps, and record label execs via a CD, DVD, USB flash drive or just send via email.

PRODUCER—The person who coordinates the production of your music recordings. There are also TV producers, who oversee the production of TV concerts and specials, and tour producers, who coordinate your concert tours.

PUBLICIST—A professional who helps singers or bands to get news stories, TV shows, etc.

PUBLICITY—Promotion of you or your band, with a press kit, fliers, social media, interviews, word of mouth, and possibly the help of a publicist.

PUNK—As in punk rock music, a genre of hard-edged rock music whose superstars of the past and present include the Ramones, the Clash, Patti Smith, the Misfits, Sleater-Kinney, the Distillers, and Green Day.

R&B—As in rhythm and blues music, a genre of music that includes everything from Motown artists and pop music to soul and gospel, and whose superstars of the past and present include Count Basie, Little Richard, Fats Domino, Nat "King" Cole, Etta James, Chuck Berry, Aretha Franklin, Sam Cooke, Marvin Gaye, Smokey Robinson, the Supremes, Diana Ross, Lionel Richie, Al Green, Stevie Wonder, Earth, Wind & Fire, the Spinners, Michael Jackson, Babyface, and Usher.

RAP—As in rap music, a genre of music that is often talked about in conjunction with hip-hop, and whose superstars of the past and present include the Sugarhill Gang, LL Cool J, the Beastie Boys, Timbaland, Nelly, and Jay-Z.

RECORD DEAL—A deal in which a record company will pay you to make a CD, which they will pay for and release on their record label. You will then receive royalties for the songs and CDs of your music that are sold.

RIDER—When you sign a contract to tour, the rider is the portion of the contract in which you can make special requests, such as certain food, drinks, or personal items you'd like to be present at the concert venue when you show up to perform. Legendary rock group Van Halen was among the first bands to add riders to their contracts, and the group also has the most famous rider in music history. To make sure the concert venue representatives were really paying attention to what they put in the rider, Van Halen requested bowls of M&M's candies to be put in their dressing rooms. But not all M&M's—the band members wanted the venue reps to make sure all the brown M&M's were removed from the bowls!

ROCK—As in rock music, the genre of music whose superstars of the past and present include Elvis Presley, the Beatles, the Who, Jimi Hendrix, the Rolling Stones, the Grateful Dead, Eric Clapton, Janis Joplin, Led Zeppelin, Bruce Springsteen, Pink Floyd, the Eagles, Van Halen, Bon Jovi, Stone Temple Pilots, Nirvana, Queen, KISS, U2, Foo Fighters, 30 Seconds to Mars, Nickelback, Linkin Park, and Kings of Leon.

***ROLLING STONE* MAGAZINE**—The leading consumer music magazine, with news, features, reviews, and interviews covering the hottest musicians in every genre.

ROYALTY—The artist's portion of payment generated from music sales.

SET—A performance.

SET LIST—The line-up of songs an artist performs during a show.

SOCIAL MEDIA PROMOTION—Using KIDZ BOP and other online sites to promote you or your band. Many, like Facebook, Twitter, Tumblr, and YouTube, have age requirements, so check with your parents before you check them out.

SOLO ARTIST—As opposed to performing as a member of a band, a solo artist performs on his or her own, usually accompanied by a back-up band, singers, or dancers. Kings of Leon, for example, is a band, but Lady Gaga is a solo artist, even though her performances include back-up singers and dancers.

SONGWRITER—A musician who writes songs. Sometimes he or she also performs, but not all songwriters are also performers.

SOUND CHECK—A performance warm-up during which a singer or band tests their equipment and its setup, as well as their voices, before officially beginning a performance in front of an audience.

STAGE PRESENCE—An artist's skill during a performance. The more dynamic the stage presence is, the better the performance will be. Think about your favorite performers; aren't they the ones who sing and dance and show an emotional connection to the song they're singing and engage with the audience? And the ones who simply stand onstage and sing? Not so entertaining, right?

STYLE—Your personal preference for clothing and accessories, as well as the haircut you sport, the way you wear makeup, and your personal grooming habits.

STYLIST—A professional fashion expert who will help you select clothing, accessories, and hair and makeup styles to bring together the look and image you want to project. Some celebs use stylists such as Rachel Zoe for everything from their everyday clothes to special gowns for awards shows and costumes for their stage performances. Other stars go the DIY route and pick out all of their own clothing and put their looks together themselves.

VOCAL COACH—A voice coach who can help you strengthen your vocals in general or specifically to fit a certain style, genre, or even a specific song. Most successful singers, even those at the superstar level, continue to work with vocal coaches even after they've sold millions of records.

The Pop Star Timeline: A Brief History of Pop Stars

Whether you look to them for inspiration or for cues on what not to do as you begin your own pop star career, here's a rundown on the history of the musical genre that just might include you as its next superstar!

THE PAST...

The 1950s

Rosemary Clooney, the aunt of future Oscar-winner George Clooney, has her first number-one hit with the song "Come on-a My House," launching her career as one of the first female pop stars. The song was written by Ross Bagdasarian, who also created Alvin and the Chipmunks.

Elvis Presley records "That's All Right" at Sun Studios in Memphis, Tennessee, starting a career that will not only lead him to becoming the King of Rock 'n' Roll, but also helping to kick off the dominance of pop and rock music around the world, and paving the way for future superstars like the Beatles.

Rock will really explode the following year, but 1955 included the release of Chuck Berry's rockin' "Maybelline" and Bill Haley and His Comets' hit "Rock Around the Clock," infectious tunes that were particularly popular with younger audiences.

One of the biggest years in music history, 1956 was the year Elvis became a superstar singer and actor. He had his first number-one hit, "Heartbreak Hotel," made his first TV appearances (including performing "Hound Dog" on *The Milton Berle Show* and causing a mini-scandal because he swiveled his hips), and signed a deal with Paramount Pictures to star in three movies, including his first, *Love Me Tender*.

The 1960s

The Miracles have a hit single with the song "Shop Around," making it the first major hit for the R&B studio Motown, which would go on to dominate much of the decade in pop music with superstars like Smokey Robinson (lead singer of the Miracles), Diana Ross and the Supremes, Marvin Gaye, Stevie Wonder, Mary Wells, and Martha and the Vandellas.

"Be My Baby," by the Ronettes, becomes one of the first, and biggest, pop hits produced by Phil Spector with his "Wall of Sound" technique, which involved recording acoustic and electronic versions of the music, as well as using instruments usually used in orchestral music, and layering them to create a richer, fuller sound that really popped on the radio. Other Wall of Sound hits: "Da Doo Ron Ron" by the Crystals, the Righteous Brothers' "Unchained Melody," and the Beatles' "The Long and Winding Road."

James Brown records and releases the album *Live at the Apollo*, which spent more than a year on the *Billboard* pop music chart and sold so well that many record stores couldn't keep it in stock. Considered one of the seminal pop/R&B and live albums, *Live at the Apollo*, Brown's other music, and his spectacular showmanship, influenced future pop stars like Michael Jackson, Mick Jagger, and Prince.

The Beatles, the British band that was already popular in Europe, first appears in the United States, and performs on *The Ed Sullivan Show*, setting off Beatlemania in the United States. After appearing on the Sullivan show three times throughout February 1964, the Beatles musical dominance in America becomes so great that, later in the year, *Billboard* proclaims that 60 percent of all record single sales belong to the British superstars. At the end of March 1964, the Beatles' songs "She Loves You," "I Want to Hold Your Hand," "Twist and Shout," and "Please Please Me" hold the top four positions on the *Billboard* pop charts.

Bob Dylan releases "Like a Rolling Stone," a song that some fans initially booed him for because they said the song's rock-ier sound meant Dylan was betraying his folk music past. The song went on to become his signature tune, however, and is considered by most rock critics and historians to be one of the most important songs ever recorded. In a 2004 issue of *Rolling Stone* magazine that featured the mag's picks for the 500 Greatest Songs of All Time, "Like a Rolling Stone" was number one.

British rock band the Who release "My Generation," a rock anthem about being misunderstood by the older generation. The song is one of the band's first American hits, and becomes one of their signature tunes. *Rolling Stone* will later out it at number 11 on its list of the 500 Greatest Songs of All Time.

The Rolling Stones, another band included in the "British Invasion" of American pop music, had their first number-one hit in the United States.

The Beach Boys release an album including songs such as "God Only Knows," "Wouldn't It Be Nice" and "Caroline, No." The 1966 album is not an overwhelming commercial success at the time, but it will go on to be included on most critics' and rock historians' lists of the greatest albums of all time. The pop album also heavily influenced other musical superstars, including Eric Clapton, Paul McCartney, Bob Dylan, and Elton John.

On a farm in upstate New York, **the Woodstock music festival** is held, drawing half a million music fans to get soaked in rain and mud while checking out performances by Joan Baez; Arlo Guthrie; Santana;

the Grateful Dead; Janis Joplin; the Who; Creedence Clearwater Revival; Crosby Stills Nash and Young; and Jimi Hendrix. Though more than double, and by some accounts triple, the number of people originally expected showed up, Woodstock is notable for remaining a mostly peaceful event.

The 1970s

Bob Marley and the Wailers release "No Woman, No Cry," bringing reggae to the mainstream and making Marley the only reggae artist to achieve international superstardom, even though the genre continues to influence pop artists today.

The Bee Gees release the soundtrack for a John Travolta dance movie, and the disco craze is officially born. Though some music purists see disco as a cheesy spin-off of pop music, the album *Saturday Night Fever* became one of the biggest selling of all time, won several Grammy awards, and spawned hit singles that remain classics today, including "How Deep Is Your Love," "Night Fever," "If I Can't Have You," and "Stayin' Alive."

The 1980s

MTV debuts, making music videos just as popular, if not more so in some cases, as music itself throughout the 1980s.

Michael Jackson releases *Thriller*, a pop music masterpiece that goes on to become the bestselling album of all time, with as many as 100 million copies sold worldwide. Seven of the album's nine songs are released as singles, Jackson dominates the music charts, his music videos revolutionize the way music videos are produced, and he earns the title "King of Pop." He also influences every aspect of popular culture, from dance to fashion, and, with his music and performances, inspires nearly every pop musician that comes after him, including current artists like Justin Timberlake, Usher, and Justin Bieber.

Bruce Springsteen becomes a huge commercial success as the rocker adds more pop flavor to his sound.

Madonna bursts onto the music scene, launching her career as a music superstar and pop culture influencer. No other female pop star in history has had the musical, music video, concert tour, and fashion influence that Madonna has had, and continues to have, in the past three—continuing into a fourth—decade.

Prince solidifies his positions as a pop/R&B superstar with four top 10 *Billboard* hit singles.

More than 2 billion viewers across the world watch the LIVE AID concert—with live performances broadcast from London and Philadelphia—in which the music industry's top artists come together to raise money for African famine relief efforts. Nearly $300 million would be raised while fans tuned in to see Paul McCartney, Sting, Elvis Costello, Phil Collins, U2, David Bowie, Queen, George Michael, the Who, Madonna, the Beach Boys, Rick Springfield, the Four Tops, Hall and Oates, Eric Clapton, Duran Duran, the Rolling Stones, and Led Zeppelin perform.

Whitney Houston becomes the new queen of pop/R&B with the release of her self-titled CD, which sells 25 million copies world-wide. Throughout her career, Houston has sold more than 100 million

CDs worldwide, including 44 million copies of the bestselling movie soundtrack of all time.

Janet Jackson releases "What Have You Done for Me Lately" and sells more than 15 million copies worldwide, starting her on the path to eventually selling more than 100 million records around the world and joining big brother Michael as a pop superstar.

Hip-hop flourishes in the 1980s, seeing its first mainstream successes, as well as the emergence of several popular sub-genres.

The 1990s

Mariah Carey releases her self-titled debut CD, and goes on to win five Grammys, record eighteen number-one singles and sell hundreds of millions of albums worldwide. As of 2010, Carey remains one of the industry's reigning pop divas.

Seattle grunge rock band **Nirvana** sets off a wave of grunge rock, also known under the genre "alternative" or "alt" rock, releases, which dominate the music industry for the first half of the '90s. Nirvana lead singer Kurt Cobain becomes the new rock icon as their first album goes on to sell 10 million copies.

The Spice Girls, a British female pop group, release their first album and will go on to become the bestselling girl group of all time, with 75 million albums sold. They also star in a movie, inspire tie-in merchandise like dolls and videogames, and earn the loyalty of teen girls all across the world with their "Girl Power!" philosophy. The individual members— Posh Spice (Victoria Beckham), Baby Spice (Emma Bunton), Scary Spice

(Melanie Brown), Ginger Spice (Geri Halliwell), and Sporty Spice (Melanie Chisholm)—go on to become international celebrities who wield influence in the music, fashion, and pop culture worlds.

The Backstreet Boys launch a self-titled debut album that will kick off a teen pop phenomenon in the late '90s. The group, with singles like "I'll Never Break Your Heart" and "Quit Playing Games (With My Heart)," will go on to sell more than 100 million albums.

'N Sync releases its self-titled debut album, with the hit singles "I Want You Back" and "Tearing Up My Heart," on the way to becoming the third most successful boy band of all time, and helping launch Justin Timberlake on a career path as one of Hollywood's biggest triple threats as a singer, dancer, and actor (not to mention songwriter and fashion designer).

On the heels of the boy band success of the Backstreet Boys and 'N Sync, Louisiana native **Britney Spears** releases her debut CD, . . . *Baby One More Time*, and becomes the biggest female pop star since Madonna (who, of course, is one of Britney's musical heroes). The album sold more than 36 million copies worldwide and remains Spears's biggest hit, though her career and personal life continue to keep her among the most popular music industry stars.

...PRESENT...

The 2000s

Pink releases her second CD, and becomes a new, edgier female pop star with songs like "Get The Party Started" and "Don't Let Me Get Me."

Justin Timberlake releases his much-anticipated debut solo CD—including the singles "Cry Me a River" and "Señorita"—which sells millions of copies and earns him two Grammy Awards.

Beyoncé Knowles releases her debut solo CD and its chart-topping lead single, "Crazy in Love." She wins five Grammy Awards and earns her status as the new queen of R&B/pop.

Usher releases a new CD including the song "Caught Up." Though he's already sold millions of records worldwide, 2004 is his most successful ever: He sells more than 20 million copies worldwide, solidifying him as the bestselling male R&B/pop artist.

American Idol season one winner **Kelly Clarkson**, hip-hop pop group Black Eyed Peas, British alt rockers Coldplay, country band Rascal Flatts, and hip-hop star Kanye West join Mariah Carey in having the bestselling albums of the year, making for a welcome diversity of musical genres at the top of the pop music charts.

American Idol winner **Carrie Underwood** and *American Idol* fourth-place finisher **Chris Daughtry** release CDs and become two of the show's most successful artists ever. Also this year is the debut CD of future country/pop crossover superstar Taylor Swift. On TV, *Hannah Montana* debuts on the Disney Channel and makes its singing lead actress, Miley Cyrus, an instant pop star.

More new pop stars arrive on the scene, most notably **Rihanna**, who soars into pop/R&B superstardom, thanks to "Umbrella" (ella, ella).

Lady Gaga becomes a global pop superstar with the release of her debut CD, *The Fame*, and her elaborate stage shows and over-the-top pop culture costumes (including one made entirely of Kermit the Frogs). And one of the most unlikely pop stars in recent history makes her debut: Forty-eight-year-old Susan Boyle wows viewers with her performance on the British reality TV series *Britain's Got Talent*, and releases her debut CD, *I Dreamed a Dream*, at the end of the year. The CD sold more than 9 million copies worldwide in its first six weeks of release.

And still more new pop stars emerge with fantastic music, great performances, and trend-setting fashion styles, including Justin Bieber, Bruno Mars, and Katy Perry, whose second album, *Teenage Dream*, debuted at number one on the *Billboard* album chart in 2010 and made her one of the year's biggest pop stars.

. . . AND FUTURE (INCLUDING YOU!) . . .

2011 and Beyond

Enter your name, or your band's name, here, and list your many accomplishments, hit records, sold-out tours, your hot new clothing line, the names of the music superstars you'll jam with at the MTV Awards this year . . . and, okay, maybe all of that hasn't happened yet, but this is the place and time to start dreaming big. So, your homework for tonight (yes, yes, you were promised there would be no homework after reading this book, but this is a fun assignment): Write a bio of you or your band, starting with your current bio, and adding in the details of the career you imagine you're going to have!

How Inspiring! The Essential Music Superstars You Must Know

These are the musical stars whose careers should inspire you to reach for the, well, stars, in your own musical career pursuits!

1. Elvis Presley
2. Michael Jackson
3. The Beatles
4. The Rolling Stones
5. Eric Clapton
6. Tina Turner
7. Madonna
8. Loretta Lynn
9. James Brown
10. Bob Dylan
11. Mariah Carey
12. Whitney Houston
13. Jimi Hendrix

14. Aerosmith
15. Led Zeppelin
16. Aretha Franklin
17. Stevie Wonder
18. Johnny Cash
19. Bruce Springsteen
20. Prince
21. James Taylor
22. The Who
23. Ray Charles
24. Diana Ross

How Inspiring! Music at the Movies . . . Makin' Sweet Music on the Big Screen

Singing, dancing, and trying to make their way in the sometimes heartbreaking music industry . . . that's what the characters in these movies are trying to do, and it's what they'll inspire you to want to do after you watch 'em in action!

Jailhouse Rock (1957)

Elvis Presley, at the height of his career, plays Vince Everett, an ex-convict (he was convicted for a fight he didn't start), who wants to pursue a career as a singer once he's out of jail. He meets a sneaky producer who steals his song, but, hey, he's Elvis, so of course everything works out in the end, including fame, fortune, a great career, and a beautiful woman who's also his business partner.

A Hard Day's Night (1964)

This comedy/mockumentary, made while Beatlemania was in full force, stars the Beatles in a silly but fun plot that follows them as they embark on a trip to London for a TV concert. The black-and-white flick gave fans a chance to see the musicians in a different light, and, of course, the soundtrack was loaded with classic Beatles tunes, including "Can't Buy Me Love," "She Loves You," "And I Love Her," and the title tune.

The Buddy Holly Story (1978)

The Oscar-winning movie tells the story of '50s rocker Buddy Holly, who was a big part of the growing popularity of rock-and-roll music, but who died in 1959 in a plane crash while on his way to a performance in Minnesota.

Grease (1978)

John Travolta is high schooler Danny Zuko, a greaser who falls in love with sweet Sandy (Olivia Newton-John) during summer vacation. He's shocked to find out she's the new student at Rydell High when the new school year begins, and they spend much of the movie singing, dancing, and alternately flirting with and ignoring each other, until the rockin' finale.

Footloose (1984)

A killer soundtrack, hot dance moves, and the adorable Kevin Bacon make this a fun flick, about a big-city teenager who moves to a small town where (gasp!) dancing and rock music aren't allowed. Bonus: A very young Sarah Jessica Parker also stars in the movie, which is being remade, starring *Dancing with the Stars* fave Julianne Hough, for release in 2011.

That Thing You Do! (1996)

Tom Hanks wrote, directed, and costars in this sweet tale about a small-town band of high school friends who become overnight pop stars. Prepare to have the movie's theme song—"That Thing You Do"—stuck in your head for weeks.

Dreamgirls (2006)

American Idol alum Jennifer Hudson won an Oscar for this musical biography, based loosely on the real-life story of Motown divas Diana Ross and the Supremes.

Hairspray (2007)

This bubbly musical stars Nikki Blonsky as Tracy; Amanda Bynes as her BFF, Penny; John Travolta as Tracy's mom; and the dreamy Zac Efron as the dreamy Link Larkin, *The Corny Collins Show* dancer who thinks Tracy is sweet!

Camp Rock (2008)

Demi Lovato and the Jonas Brothers star in this Disney Channel gem about an aspiring singer (Lovato) and the pop star (Joe Jonas) who falls in love with her when they both spend the summer at a music camp.

Girls Rock! The Movie (2008)

The documentary follows the real-life girls who attend the real-life version of Camp Rock, the Rock and Roll Camp for Girls, in Portland, Oregon.

Rock Star Chic

Nothing is more important than the music . . . that is why you're getting into the business, right? But it's also undeniable that audiences want their pop stars to be interesting, to have style, flair, cool haircuts, outrageous clothes, and signature accessories. Justin Bieber wouldn't be Justin Bieber without the bangs and the hats. Lady Gaga wouldn't be Lady Gaga without the sky-high shoes, the meat dresses, and the masks. Beyoncé wouldn't be Beyoncé without the glam hair and makeup and the sparkly designer outfits that show off her impossibly long legs. You get the idea . . . these are things we associate with each of these pop stars because they're part of their personal styles . . . it's what gives them their rock star, pop star flair!

What will your style be? Do you love wearing dresses or skirts? Maybe, like the Biebs, it's jeans, Ts, and fun jackets for you? Do you like to wear outrageous colors, or mix patterns and styles that don't seem to go together (until you put your spin on them and turn them into an eye-catching ensemble)? Do you wear a different hairstyle every day?

If you're trying to cultivate a personal style, a style that will make you pop star chic, here are a few tips to help you:

How Inspiring! Ten Places to Find Inspiration for Your Signature Style

1. Magazines. *Vogue, Elle, Rolling Stone, Seventeen, Teen Vogue, People, US Weekly, Spin* . . . go through the pages and look at the photos, the ads, the fashion features, what the celebs are wearing. Tear out pages of things that interest and inspire you and save them in an idea folder!
2. Ditto Websites. Check out sites like KIDZ BOP, Teen.com, Seventeen.com . . . notice what people are wearing, the colors you like, the styles you like, the accessories that catch your eye. Again, print out pages of things that inspire you, that you think you can put a fresh spin on and make your own.
3. Don't limit yourself to what you already know. Forever 21 and Hollister may be your go-to spots for shopping, but consider other places. Browse in stores at the mall you might not go into otherwise. Ask people you know whose style is different from yours, but whose look you find interesting, where they shop. Be open to trying new things that might flatter you.
4. Vintage clothing stores, Goodwill, yard sales, your aunt/older sibling/parents/grandma and grandpa's storage boxes. One of the big truisms in fashion is that everything old is new again, which means every fashion fad, no matter how outrageous, is probably going to come back into style at some point. Legwarmers and Madonna's jelly bracelets

from the '80s . . . jumpsuits from the '70s . . . miniskirts and hippie gear from the '60s . . . they've all had comebacks since they were originally popular, and those fads, and many more, will come back again. Maybe you're even the one who will help usher them back into vogue?

5. Creating a personal style isn't just about what clothes and accessories you own . . . it's also about how you wear them. Kiddie hip-hoppers Kris Kross famously wore their pants backwards in the '90s. Celine Dion once wore a white tuxedo jacket backwards (to the Oscars!). And during Michael Jackson's *Thriller* video days, he wore pants tailored to be too short, showing off his glittery socks. We're not suggesting you wear all your clothes backwards or wear high-water pants, but you could put a DIY spin on some of your duds. Personalize your jeans with some bedazzling action. Use fabric paint to paint a mini mural on your Chuck Taylors. Visit a craft store for some beads and fashion your own necklaces, rings, bracelets, headbands, and earrings. Turn long T-shirts into dresses over colored tights and a wide belt to give it shape. Wrap a long necklace around your wrist several times to turn it into a cool, layered bracelet. Old jeans . . . there are tons of DIY instructions on the web to show you how to turn them into a new skirt.

6. Take a sewing class at a local craft store, or ask someone who already knows how to sew to teach you. It's one of the best skills you can have, especially for creating fabulous fashions on a budget and being able to do your own alterations exactly when you need them.

7. Spend an afternoon at a bookstore flipping through magazines, fashion books, giant coffee-table books on Hollywood style and glamour, books on rock and roll history . . . all great sources of style inspiration.

8. Channel surf. Click through Nickelodeon, TeenNick, E!, the Style network, CMT, old movies, and classic TV shows on TV Land. It's a great place to see fashions from other times in history, as well as hot current fashions. Check out shows like *Project Runway* to see how a clothing designer's creative process works.

9. Don't forget to check out hairstyles while you're looking through all those magazines, books, movies, TV shows, and websites. A person's hair can be their signature (again, Justin Bieber's bangs come to mind), and it can also be a versatile instrument in changing your look from time to time.

10. One word: shoes. Many an outfit has been made great by a pair of incredible shoes, just as many an outfit has been ruined by the wrong ones. Incredible shoes can be a big part of your style—who doesn't love to see Gaga tottering around in her Alexander McQueen armadillo boots, for example? Of course, comfort should play at least a small role in all your fashion decisions, especially when, as a pop star, you'll be on your feet, in your stage clothes, a lot. So, while we love watching Gaga in her mile-high boots, we wouldn't actually want to be the ones trying to get through an international airport, quickly, with lots of luggage, followed by paparazzi, while wearing them.

Pop Star Style: Dos and Don'ts for Girls

★ **DO:** Look to others for inspiration and ideas for creating your own style.

★ **DON'T:** Totally copy anyone's look. Creating your personal style should be just that . . . personal. If you copy someone else's look, that makes it their personal style on your body, and that's no fun. You're a creative, unique person, and that's what you want to convey in your music and your pop star style!

★ **DO:** Always make sure your look, your clothing, is appropriate and flattering on you.

★ **DON'T:** Dress like you're twenty-one or wear too-tight clothing, just because it's what some celebrities do. You've seen it on other people, so you know it's true: Nothing makes for a bigger fashion disaster than someone wearing clothing that's too old for the person or too tight.

★ **DO:** Wear pretty accessories, like jewelry, hats, belts, and stylish eyewear.

★ **DON'T:** Overdo it. You don't want to look like a Christmas tree.

★ **DO:** Make note of fashion trends, especially the ones that will be flattering to you.

★ **DON'T:** Be a fashion slave. Don't simply buy a complete outfit off a store mannequin because it looks great on the mannequin. Make sure things look good on you, specifically. And the same goes for trendy makeup and hairstyles. Visit a department store makeup counter for help in picking out what works best for your skin and your features, and talk to your hair stylist about what is flattering for your hair length, texture, color, and face, as well as what kind of cut works best for your lifestyle.

Pop Star Style: Dos and Don'ts for Guys

★ **DO:** Wear clothing that fits well and is flattering to your body.

★ **DON'T:** Wear clothes that are too baggy. Or too tight. Neither will make you look like the adorable young rocker that you are.

★ **DO:** Be stylish, and choose from fashion trends that help you convey the image you want to convey.

★ **DON'T:** Copy your heroes. Just because your favorite rocker wears a certain brand of sneaker or paints his fingernails black doesn't mean you should.

★ **DO:** Make an effort.

★ **DON'T:** Again, just because you're a guy, don't throw on your oldest jeans and most comfy T-shirt and declare that your style. Think about the styles you like and are comfortable with and that look good on you and fit your personality. Consider getting a great haircut. Find an accessory—a cool watch, hat, color—that you love and make it part of your signature look. Having a rock star style means making sure everything about you, from your music to your look, lets the people you're working with, the people who will help promote you or your band, and your fans know who you are.

★ **DO:** Be willing to try something different.

★ **DON'T:** Go overboard. No one's suggesting you wear a glitter suit or fifty pounds of chains around your neck. But if you are the guy who happily goes through life in jeans, Ts, and sneakers, consider going a little upscale with your look. Instead of old, worn jeans, try a pair of nice-fitting, stylish, dark wash jeans. A great shirt and jacket combo. Sharp hair, styled, with product. Dark shoes that you have to actually lace up, not your old Nikes that are so worn you can take them off and put them on without tying or untying them.

Superstar Stylin' on a DIY Budget

Because until you're actually making those rock star dollars you don't want to spend rock star money on your clothing, right?

1. Clothing swaps! You and your friends get together, and everyone brings gently used clothing that they no longer want, or, at least, are willing to part with in exchange for other stuff. Put names in a hat, pull them out one at a time, and when your name is chosen, you get to choose something "new." Make it even more fun and invite friends and relatives who go to other schools, so you know everyone has a chance to get cool clothes and accessories they haven't seen before. It's like shopping, for free!

2. If you have a favorite place to shop, go to the store's website and sign up for any free VIP shopping clubs or coupon offers. This can get you regular coupons for big savings at your favorite stores!

3. Also, ask your mom to check out coupon websites like Retailmenot .com, Fatwallet.com, and Couponcabin.com for online shopping codes and printable coupons. As an example, you can regularly find

40 percent–off coupons for Justice clothing stores at the coupon websites.

4. Vintage clothing stores can be a goldmine!

5. As can Goodwill and consignment shops!

6. Customize your old clothes with paint, bows, ribbons, rhinestones, and other goodies from the craft store. Those super-expensive designer jeans with rips and tears and faded spots and rhinestone trims? All stuff you can do yourself by starting with an inexpensive, but well-fitting pair of jeans, plus scissors, a bit of sandpaper, and more goodies from the craft store!

7. Dye your own clothes. Make sure you read the instructions very carefully—and, more importantly, make sure you have your parents' permission to get creative in their washing machine. But a few bucks for a box of dye can turn old pants and shirts into fab and funky fashions!

8. Don't underestimate how well accessories can pull a look together. A great necklace or shoes can really make an outfit, and cool add-ons like funky costume jewelry is always available at discounted prices at flea markets, yard sales, and discount stores.

KIDZ BOP KIDS ON: ROCK STAR STYLE

STEFFAN: "My number-one priority is to be comfortable, but I also like to look good, so if I feel like wearing a hoodie, I wear a nice shirt underneath it. Or I'll wear jeans, but with a nice shirt and a funky tie. Cool and comfortable!"

HANNA: "My thing is wearing my hair in ponytails, so I always look for cute hair accessories. And, because you can always see my earrings when my hair is pulled back, I have tons of pretty little earrings, in every color you can think of."

EVA: "I'm a big fan of colorful clothes and jewelry, so I wear a lot of bright sweaters, bright colors like pink on my fingernails, and cool jewelry in bold colors. I also love scarves, and have them to go with all my outfits."

ELIJAH: "I live in sneakers, but not just boring regular ones. I have them in red, turquoise, all kinds of colors."

CHARISMA: "I'm a girly girl, and I can't get enough pink and purple in my wardrobe. Purple skirts, pink sweaters, pink and purple flats . . . I love them!"

Glam Grooming 101

We'll get right to the point on this one, because we all know it's true: Funky is great when you're describing someone's clothing, but most definitely not when you're describing someone's breath, fingernails, or general state of hygiene. So, as we prepare to close out this chapter on preparing to embark on pursuing your pop star dreams, we'll keep this section on grooming short and sweet!

What a Diva Needs to Know

1. Teeth: are they brushed and free of food particles? Check!
2. Breath: is it sweet and minty fresh? Check!
3. Fingernails: are they neatly trimmed? If they're long, are they shaped nicely? And, if they're painted, are they free of chipped polish? Check!
4. Deodorant: are you wearing some? Because being a pop diva is a demanding, physical job, and it's gonna make you perspire. So, deodorant? Check!
5. Hair: clean and styled? Check!
6. Clothing: clean, pressed, free of stains and holes? Check!
7. Skin: clean, lotioned, no dry or cracked patches? Check!

8. Lips: moisturized? Check!

9. Perfume: wearing some? Cool. Not wearing any? Also cool. Wearing so much you're making those around you sneeze? Not cool. Apply with a light touch? Check!

10. Makeup: if you're performing, then wearing makeup makes sense. But offstage, all you really need is lip gloss!

What a Guitar Hero Needs to Know

1. Shower: you've been in one today? Check!

2. Teeth: are they brushed and free of food particles? Check!

3. Breath: is it sweet and minty fresh? Check!

4. Fingernails: no dirt underneath them? No jagged hangnails? Check!

5. Lips: moisturized? Check!

6. Clothing: clean, pressed, free of stains and holes? Check!

7. Hair: clean and styled? Check!

8. Cologne: wearing some? Cool. Not wearing any? Also cool. Wearing so much you're making those around you sneeze? Not cool. Apply with a light touch? Check!

9. Deodorant: are you wearing some? Because being a guitar hero is a demanding, physical job, and it's gonna make you sweat. So, deodorant? Check!

10. Socks and undergarments: fresh ones today? We know, it's a guy thing, but no recycling, right? Check!

KIDZ BOP KIDS ON: GLAM GROOMING

STEFFAN: "I actually prefer it when girls don't wear a lot of makeup or use a lot of perfume."

HANNA: "I carry a toothbrush and toothpaste with me in my bag, because sometimes, when we're super busy, we have to grab lunch or a snack really quickly, and I want to be able to brush afterward, especially if I ate something with onions."

EVA: "I love it when guys wear cologne. But not too much!"

ELIJAH: "I think everyone, guys and girls, smell best when they don't use lots of perfume or cologne, and just smell clean. But everyone definitely needs to use deodorant. No one smells better without that."

CHARISMA: "I never leave home without ChapStick (cherry flavor) and lip gloss (also cherry flavor!)."

PART TWO

CHAPTER 2
KIDZ BOP Pop Princess

"I WANT TO BE BOLD, DARING, FEARLESS. I'M NOT AFRAID TO BE ADVENTUR-OUS. I THINK WE ALL INSPIRE EACH OTHER."

—RIHANNA

It's good to be queen. And that's what you'll be when you're a pop princess, joining the ranks of such music royalty as Kelly Clarkson, Selena Gomez, and Rihanna. These are the regal performers who know who they are—and work it to the max.

Pop princesses live the glam dream from head to toe. Everybody loves them—and everybody wants to be them. Starting with you! The difference is, you've got the talent and the drive and the smarts to go from princess-in-training to real-life pop princess!

You know that you were born to be a pop princess if you:

★ Have one and only one goal—to be a star!
★ Never think twice about where you've been, only where you're going
★ Dream about playing Madison Square Garden
★ Think the perfect triple-threat concert would be Beyoncé with Madonna and Mariah Carey
★ Can play an instrument—or not
★ Own the stage whenever you step on it

★ Sing like an angel and dance like a rocker
★ Strut like you already are somebody—because you are!

Power to the Pop Princess!

> "I STOOD IN FRONT OF SONY (MUSIC HEADQUARTERS) OUT HERE, I STOOD RIGHT IN FRONT OF THE BUILDING WITH A JAM BOX AND A TAPE PLAYER, SINGING MY HEART OUT."
>
> —KELLY CLARKSON

There's something that separates pop princesses from the rest of the singers in the world: confidence. If you're a pop princess, you are blessed with an unshakable belief in yourself—and that gives you the guts to go for what you want. You see obstacles as opportunities—and that makes all the difference.

IN THE KIDZ BOP POP PRINCESS SPOTLIGHT

Barbados native Rihanna now reigns supreme as a pop princess—but it wasn't always that way. Her first couple of albums showcased her Caribbean roots; yet critics were lukewarm about the dance hall and reggae-style tunes and ballads. Rihanna rebelled against this typecasting, and with true queenly intuition cut off her hair and dyed it black to reflect her new independence.

The result: "Umbrella," the single heard around the world, and her most critically acclaimed and bestselling album to date. "I want to keep people dancing, but still be soulful at the same time," Rihanna said at the time—and she succeeded beyond all expectations. Except her own!

Play to Your People

> "THE DAY I GOT MY FIRST LETTER FROM A FAN, I FELT LIKE I'D BEEN TOUCHED BY AN ANGEL. I OPENED THE NOTE AND READ EVERY SINGLE WORD THE FAN, TAYLOR, HAD TO SAY. . . . I ALMOST CRIED. I WROTE HER BACK THIS REALLY LONG LETTER WITH AN AUTOGRAPH TO SHOW HER HOW SWEET I THOUGHT SHE WAS."
>
> —SELENA GOMEZ

A true pop princess appreciates her fans—and gives them credit for acknowledging her star power and supporting her career. So she signs autographs and gives interviews, and is happy to do it!

As a pop princess yourself, you owe it to your fans to do the same. And don't worry if now your biggest fan is your mom. That will change—and soon! Your fan base will grow as you grow as a performer. Just be sure that you maintain a connection with your fans, through websites like KIDZ BOP and fan clubs and appearances and more. Why? Because you know that a pop princess needs an audience to really shine.

Make a Rockin' KIDZ BOP Pop Princess Video!

The general rule of thumb for a pop princess video: It's all about *you*! Pop princesses are the center of attention by divine right. The camera loves you—and you love the camera. It's a mutual admiration society!

If you're a pop princess, you know that your music video is your royal calling card—and you won't settle for anything less than truly fab! So plan your videos with care down to the latest detail—from the first frame to the last:

★ Start with a setting as awesome as you are—whether it's a beach or a bistro, a meadow or a mall, a boutique or a ballpark. Make it a backdrop where you will stand out, even if you have to paint it yourself!

★ Wear a great outfit worthy of a pop princess, one that suits you as well as the theme of your music video.

★ Choose a number that highlights your strengths as a performer and reflects your own unique personality.

Let your authenticity shine through—just like the pop princess you are!

KIDZ BOP NOTES

Cyndi Lauper took home the first MTV award for best female video for the pop princess classic "Girls Just Want to Have Fun."

Pop Princess Music Videos

Here are KIDZ BOP Kid Eva's Five Faves:

1. "Umbrella" by Rihanna
2. "A Year Without Rain" by Selena Gomez
3. "Kissin U" by Miranda Cosgrove
4. "Here We Go Again" by Demi Lovato
5. "Holiday" by Hilary Duff

Your KIDZ BOP Pop Princess Backup Band

As a pop princess, you belong front and center. You're versatile enough to perform with virtually any band, any time. You may be part of a band, but if you are, you're the lead singer—and your band understands that you're the star and that their job is to make you look good.

That said, you're prepared to perform wherever and whenever an opportunity presents itself—whether that's at a karaoke party or in a church choir or a school talent show. You're always ready to make an impression—and win some more fans!

KIDZ BOP Pop Princess Set List

The perfect pop princess set list is one that spotlights your unique gifts *and* draws a crowd. Here are some classics that are guaranteed to keep the spotlight on you!

- ★ "Oops! . . . I Did It Again" by Britney Spears
- ★ "What a Girl Wants" by Christina Aguilera
- ★ "I Think I'm in Love with You" by Jessica Simpson
- ★ "Because of You" by Kelly Clarkson
- ★ "Miss You Much" by Janet Jackson
- ★ "Fallin'" by Alicia Keys
- ★ "Crazy for You" by Madonna
- ★ "Breathe" by Faith Hill
- ★ "Un-break My Heart" by Toni Braxton
- ★ "You're Still the One" by Shania Twain

The Pop Princess BFF Club

Demi Lovato and Selena Gomez have been best friends since they were just little kids on the set of *Barney and Friends*. It's a bond they can count on—and fame and fortune didn't change it. Demi even wrote a song celebrating their friendship, called "Two Worlds Collide."

Every pop princess needs a BFF of her own. So find yourself a confidante and true-blue bud you can hang with as you make your way up the charts. And if she's a pop princess herself, all the better!

> "I'M LUCKY BECAUSE ALL OF MY FRIENDS ARE FROM ELEMENTARY SCHOOL, SO THEY JUST SEE ME AS THE SAME DORKY MIRANDA THAT THEY KNEW BEFORE."
>
> —MIRANDA COSGROVE

Write a Pop Princess Hit

> "I'M REALLY EXCITED ABOUT THESE SONGS. I FEEL LIKE I'VE REALLY GROWN AS A SONGWRITER WITH MY LAST FEW SONGS, AND I'M ANXIOUS TO SEE WHAT THE FANS THINK OF THEM."
>
> —DEMI LOVATO

There's only one word for writing a pop princess hit. (Hint: It's one of your *fave* words!)

And that word is . . . drumroll . . . *boys*!

You're always talking about boys anyway, so just start writing your boy-centric musings down! From the first time you see him to your first kiss—and every exciting moment in between—it's all fair game for a song. So the next time you find yourself gabbing on and on to your girlfriends about what he just did or said, write it down!

Top 10 Topics for a KIDZ BOP Pop Princess Song

1. New love
2. Old love
3. Why you're better off without him
4. Shopping for fun and wardrobe
5. Who needs boys, anyway
6. Hanging with your BFF

7. Breaking up
8. Making up
9. It's great to be a girl
10. Your inner princess

Pen Your Own KIDZ BOP Pop Princess Song

Let's hear it for the boys—in your first pop hit! Fill in the blanks below, and sing your way to center stage!

It's been _____ days
                              adjective

I _____ you truly
           verb

In _____ ways
         adjective

You were so _____ to me
                        adjective

I'm so _____
               adjective

You _____
           verb

I'm so _____ and _____ without you
               adjective   adjective

Don't _____ ,
                verb

I won't _____ you
                  verb

But you'd better _____
verb

'Cause I _____ you, I really do.
verb

You thought you were so _____ , well,
adjective

I'm here to tell you

What you should _____ know
adverb

It just ain't so.

As _____ as me
adjective

But any _____ could see
noun

You are so _____ _____ to me.
adjective   _noun_

It's been _____ days
adjective

I _____ you truly
verb

In _____ ways
adjective

You were so _____ to me
adjective

I'm so _____
         adjective

You can't _____
                  verb

I'm so _____ and _____ without you.
         adjective   adjective

_____ days without you.
     adjective

_____ days without you.
     adjective

_____ days without you.
     adjective

The Princess Shopping Diaries

"I LOVE CLOTHES. I CAN'T CONTROL MYSELF. I HAVE A HUGE FETISH FOR SHOES AND CLOTHES AND MAKEUP. I'M THE KIND OF PERSON WHO DOESN'T LIKE TO WEAR THINGS OVER AND OVER AGAIN."

—HILARY DUFF

Now that's a pop princess talking!

So plan your wardrobe, and shop accordingly. Your public is depending on it.

There's a fine line between fashion-forward and freaky—and a pop princess never crosses it. You'll want to maintain a personal style that's chic and glam and fun—and you'll look great in it!

Pop Princess Wardrobe Checklist

- ★ Short skirts
- ★ Fitted dresses
- ★ Anything with a designer label
- ★ Belts
- ★ Hats
- ★ Handbags
- ★ Accessories
- ★ Shoes
- ★ Shoes
- ★ Shoes

KIDZ BOP POP PRINCESS SAYS: IT'S ALL ABOUT THE SHOES!

Selena Gomez has more than twenty pairs of Converse sneakers!

When They Were KIDZ

Once a pop princess, always a pop princess. It's never too early to realize how special you are—or understand that stardom is your destiny.

- ★ Selena Gomez and best bud Demi Lovato were both on *Barney and Friends* when they were just tots.
- ★ Rihanna began singing when she was only seven.
- ★ Miranda Cosgrove was discovered by a talent agent in an L.A. restaurant when she was three.
- ★ At six, Hilary Duff was performing *The Nutcracker* with the Columbus BalletMet in San Antonio, Texas.
- ★ Kelly Clarkson joined the school choir in the seventh grade, after a teacher overheard her singing the hall.

Anything these pop princesses can do, you can do better. Your destiny awaits, KIDZ BOP pop princess! Go for it!

KIDZ BOP KIDS ON: POP PRINCESS MOVES

CHARISMA: "I always have my music in my backpack in case I need it. It's a folder with sheet music of my fave songs in a variety of keys. Because you never know when someone's gonna ask you to perform—and I want to be ready!"

HANNA: "I have an awesome scrapbook. My mom gave it to me as a birthday present, so I can have a record of everything that happens to me on my road to stardom! I put in photos and postcards and tickets—and add stickers and glitter and lots of cool stuff. It's great to have all the memories I want to save forever in one place—and maybe someday I'll share them with my fans!"

EVA: "Clothes, shoes, makeup—it's all good! I love shopping! Being a pop princess means dressing like one—I wouldn't want to disappoint my fans!"

CHAPTER 3

KIDZ BOP Singer-Songwriter

> "I CONSIDER MYSELF A POET FIRST AND A MUSICIAN SECOND."
>
> —BOB DYLAN

Singer-songwriters are the poets of the music business—creating the quirky, offbeat, one-of-a-kind songs that resonate with people the world over. If you're a singer-songwriter, writing songs is as important to you as performing them.

Being a singer-songwriter means being a storyteller first—and second. From Paul Simon and Joni Mitchell to Sara Bareilles and Jason Mraz, these are the performers who really write the songs the world sings—and keeps on singing.

You know that you were born to be a singer-songwriter if you:

- ★ Have been writing songs ever since you could sing
- ★ Think of your guitar as your best friend
- ★ Need to express yourself the way you need to breathe
- ★ Think the perfect triple-threat concert would be James Blunt with John Mayer and Sheryl Crow
- ★ Could pick out a new song on a guitar or piano or kazoo
- ★ Have a very individualistic approach to fashion
- ★ Spend a lot of time in your room thinking, writing, and being creative

★ Love hanging out with musicians
★ Enjoy rehearsing as much as performing

Make Your Own KIDZ BOP Singer-Songwriter Magic

The coolest indie singer-songwriters make it look so easy.

You can too. All you have to do is write, compose, sing, and play great songs in that trademark low-key indie way—without seeming to break a sweat. Seriously, it can be done. The trick is to start at the beginning—with a great song.

Write an Indie Hit

"SONGWRITING IS A VERY MYSTERIOUS PROCESS. IT FEELS LIKE CREATING SOMETHING FROM NOTHING. IT'S SOMETHING I DON'T FEEL LIKE I REALLY CONTROL."

—TRACY CHAPMAN

KIDZ BOP KIDS ON: SONGWRITING

STEFFAN: "I just pick up my guitar and start fooling around, putting chords together until something clicks."

EVA: "I get my best ideas for songs when I'm doing something else—shopping with my mom or hanging out with my friends at school or going to dance class. I record notes to myself on my phone, and then later when I'm home I listen to them and see what I can do. If I get stuck, I invite my friends over and we jam until we come up with something."

HANNA: "I write a lot of poetry. A lot of it is just for me, but when I start something that I think other people might like, I make a song out of it. Then I ask Steffan to put it to music."

ELIJAH: "I'm always scribbling lyrics in my journal. I work on a song for a long time, until I get it right, and then I sit down at the piano and try to match the words to a melody."

CHARISMA: "I like to write songs with my BFF Sara back home. We get out our keyboards and improvise, singing and playing. We wrote a song for the talent show at school—and won first place!"

The process of writing a great song varies from artist to artist. You may start with the music, relying on your instrument for inspiration. Or maybe it's the words that spark your imagination, and you write the lyrics first.

"THE WRITING PROCESS FOR ME IS PRETTY MUCH ALWAYS THE SAME—IT'S A SOLITARY EXPERIENCE."

—SHERYL CROW

If you love to compose music, but you struggle with lyrics, pair up with a wordsmith—or vice versa. The music business is full of dynamic-duo songwriting teams—from the Beatles' Lennon and McCartney to Jimmy Jam and Terry Lewis, who've written hits for Mariah Carey and Janet Jackson, among others. Find yourself a songwriting partner, and get to work!

Or maybe you see songwriting as a group activity, jamming with your friends and brainstorming on the fly.

However you like to do it, just do it—because the sooner you write the songs, the sooner you can perform them!

Top 10 Topics for a KIDZ BOP Indie Song

1. Your favorite poem, written by you
2. Your favorite poem, written by someone else
3. Love is a _____
   insert metaphor here
4. Your pet
5. Your pet peeve
6. Inspiration/Inspiring a friend
7. The environment
8. The nature of the universe
9. Current events
10. World peace

Make an Indie Music Video: The KIDZ BOP WAY!

Elijah loves to shoot videos. He's always got a Flip camera in his pocket—and whenever you least expect it, he's capturing your every move! According to Elijah, there are three main ways to shoot an indie music video:

1. Keep it simple. Focus on your performance. Just grab a chair and a guitar, throw on a pair of jeans and a T-shirt, plop down in front of a white backdrop, and sing. Shoot it in black-and-white, mix close-ups and wide shots, throw in some cool fonts on the credits, and you can make indie magic—simple but sensational!
2. Go all out. Put on a musical extravaganza as weird and wonderful as any scene out of a Tim Burton movie.
3. Like Elijah says, it's up to you! You are limited only by your imagination—and creative singer-songwriters have imagination to spare!

Here are KIDZ BOP Kid Hanna's Top Ten Singer-Songwriter Music Videos:

1. "Love Song" by Sara Bareilles
2. "Make It Mine" by Jason Mraz
3. "Just the Way You Are" by Bruno Mars
4. "The Only Exception" by Paramore
5. "Decode" by Paramore
6. "Bubbly" by Colbie Caillat
7. "Hey There Delilah" by the Plain White T's
8. "Sinkin' Soon" by Norah Jones
9. "Fell in Love with a Girl" by the White Stripes
10. "Wanderlust" by Bjork

Do You Need a Backup Band?

You may be the kind of singer-songwriter who prefers to go it alone — just you and your guitar on an empty stage — with a full house in front of you. But you might think it's a lot more fun to be a part of a band. Being in a band means you're making music together — and you think you make better music that way!

That's how Hayley Williams felt. She started hanging out with Josh and Zack Farro and Jeremy Davis when they were all teenagers in Franklin, Tennessee. She signed a record deal with Atlantic Records, but refused to go solo. Instead, she and her musical pals formed the hit indie band Paramore.

KIDZ BOP Kid Hanna Says: Keep a Poetry Journal

Hanna loves to read poetry — Jewel is a favorite — and write poetry, too.

If you write poetry like KIDZ BOP Kid Hanna, keep a poetry journal. Fill it with poems — and see which you might turn into songs. If you don't write poetry, give it a try. Writing poems will sharpen your sense of language and lyricism—and you'll write better songs for it.

> "I'VE ALWAYS HAD A LOVE FOR POETRY, AND WHEN I GOT SIGNED TO A RECORD LABEL I THOUGHT, 'HOW ODD THAT I'M DOING A RECORD BEFORE A BOOK OF POETRY.'"
>
> —JEWEL

Lyrics often read like poems, Hanna says, because often they are:

★ Bob Dylan, the father of all singer-songwriters, considers all his songs poems.

★ Jewel writes and publishes songs and poems, noting that while she finds the rhythms and rhymes of each form different, they do inform one another.

★ Patti Smith gives poetry readings and concerts.

★ The classic poem *Metamorphoses* inspired British alternative rock band Keane to write the 2008 hit "Spiralling," which became their label's fastest-downloading song ever (reaching 500,000 downloads in less than a week).

Pen Your Own KIDZ BOP Indie Song

> "I JUST WRITE SONGS THAT I STRONGLY BELIEVE IN AND THAT ARE COMING FROM A SPECIAL PLACE. THERE'S NO TRICKS. . . . IT'S HONESTY."
>
> —BRUNO MARS

You, too, can write songs that come from a special place. Fill in the blanks below, and be honest!

Love is a _____
                    noun

Love is a _____
                    noun

Love is a _____
                    noun

I can't _____
                verb

What _____ **will do**
              noun

In the name of love

It's so _____ **but it's true**
                verb

Love is a _____ .
                    noun

You _____ **with me**
            verb

You _____ **with me**
         rhyming verb

You _____ **and** _____
            verb   verb

But I _____ **to see**
              verb

What you _____ **when you** _____ **me.**
                  verb   verb

There's a _____ **called** _____
                  noun   noun

Maybe you should _____
verb

Then I'd _____ **know**
adverb

How _____ **you can go**
adjective

Love is a _____ .
noun

Love is a _____
noun

Love is a _____
noun

Love is a _____
noun

I can't _____
verb

What _____ **will do**
noun

In the name of love

It's so _____ **but it's true**
adjective

Love is a _____ .
noun

Dress the Part

> "I DO TRY AND WEAR STUFF BY UNKNOWN DESIGNERS."
>
> —BJORK

When Bjork wore her infamous swan dress to the Oscars, she was doing what indie artists do—wearing whatever the heck she wanted. You can, too; the trick is to create a signature style all your own.

Singer-Songwriter Wardrobe Checklist for Girls
You can go girly or tomboy, edgy or elegant—just be sure that your style is as individual as you are.

- ★ Jeans
- ★ T-shirts
- ★ Hippie chic
- ★ Punk chic
- ★ Short skirts
- ★ Long dresses
- ★ Funky accessories
- ★ Anything vintage
- ★ Any kind of hat
- ★ Any kind of shoes or boots
- ★ Brightly colored knee socks, tights, anklets

Singer-Songwriter Wardrobe Checklist for Guys
You can dress to suit yourself, too. But do consider adopting a trademark all your own—like Bruno Mars and his trademark hats.

- ★ Jeans
- ★ T-shirts

★ Retro suits
★ Any kind of hat
★ Any kind of shoes or boots
★ Sneakers
★ Lots of hair

When They Were KIDZ

The singer-songwriter typically stands out from the crowd at an early age:

★ Bruno Mars started impersonating stars when he was little, appearing in a cameo as "Little Elvis" in *Honeymoon in Vegas* at age six.
★ As a teen, Jason Mraz played the lead role in the musical *Joseph and the Amazing Technicolor Dreamcoat*, a production put on by the School of the Performing Arts in Richmond, Virginia.
★ Hayley Williams of Paramore was a shy kid who suffered from stage fright until she started taking singing lessons at thirteen.
★ Jack White started playing his first instrument, the drums, at age six.
★ As a teenager, Colbie Caillat sang backup on techno tracks designed for fashion shows.
★ Greyson Chance performed Lady Gaga's "Paparazzi" at his sixth-grade music festival.

You know you've got a song to sing—and more where that came from. So polish up your performance and get out there and do it! And don't forget to shoot a video and post it online at KIDZ BOP . . . you could be the next KIDZ BOP Kid!

KIDZ BOP KIDS ON: THEIR FAVE SINGER-SONGWRITERS

STEFFAN: "I love 3OH!3—they're from Colorado, just like me!"

HANNA: "Selena Gomez—I think it's so awesome that she's writing her own songs now. My fave is "'I Won't Apologize.'"

ELIJAH: "Bruno Mars writes great songs—and he's got style!"

CHARISMA: "Colbie Caillat—her music is so real and so sweet."

EVA: "The Ting Tings—they're so hip and I love their English accents!"

CHAPTER 4
KIDZ BOP Country Crooner

> "COUNTRY MUSIC IS THREE CHORDS AND THE TRUTH."
>
> —HARLAN HOWARD

If you live and breathe country music, then odds are you're a down-to-earth diva or dude who just wants to have a good time making the music you love for the people you love. Country music is, as superstar Faith Hill likes to say, the "music of the people." It's an all-American kind of music!

But you don't have to be country-born to be a crooner. Some of the biggest stars in country music are from big cities or the 'burbs—like Taylor Swift, who hails from the Pittsburgh area. Many others come from foreign lands—Shania Twain from Canada and Keith Urban, who was born in New Zealand and raised in Australia, to name just two. So whether you come from a Midwestern suburb or a booming metropolis or a sleepy small town, it really doesn't matter.

You know that you were born to be a country crooner if you:

★ Write songs straight from your heart—and your life
★ Come from a small town—or just wish you did
★ Dream about playing the Grand Ole Opry
★ Think the perfect triple-threat concert would be Taylor Swift with Tim McGraw and Faith Hill

★ Play a mean guitar, banjo, and/or fiddle
★ Own more than one pair of awesome cowboy boots
★ Could go toe to toe on the dance floor with Julianne Hough
★ Can trill and twang your way through any country song
★ Love hitting those oh-so-high—and oh-so-low—notes

Choose Your KIDZ BOP Country Style

You love country, but what kind of country? There are all kinds of country music, which makes it all the more fun to discover which is best for you. Country music comes in all flavors:

★ Alternative country
★ Bluegrass
★ Contemporary country
★ Cowboy
★ Country gospel
★ Country pop
★ Country rock
★ Honky-tonk
★ Outlaw music
★ Rockabilly
★ Traditional country
★ Western swing

Experiment with these styles—and learn what each might offer you in your own quest for stardom. But remember; the biggest country stars are the ones who cross over into pop stardom—like Taylor Swift!

Make Your Own KIDZ BOP Crossover Magic

The most popular country singers make music that everybody loves, from Nashville to New York City and beyond. If you want to pull a Carrie Underwood or a Taylor Swift, a Tim McGraw or Keith Urban, then you need to max out your appeal—without losing your country roots.

Study your favorite artists, and borrow whatever you think might work for you. From Josh Turner's mellow machismo and Kellie Pickler's spunky charm to Johnny Cash's cool and Patsy Cline's soul, there's something you can learn from all the top country stars.

KIDZ BOP KID CHARISMA SAYS:

To cross over, you need to go pop! I love Taylor Swift, but Martina McBride is my hero. Martina started out singing just country. Her first three albums were big, but not *huge.* With her fourth album, *Evolution,* Martina switched to a country pop sound—and now she's known as the "Celine Dion of Country"!

Make a Rockin' KIDZ BOP Country Music Video!

The coolest music videos in this genre are country at the core—yet still cool! To make yours stand out:

★ Try an unexpected venue like a swimming pool or an art gallery or a shopping mall.
★ Go for something country but fun—like a rodeo, a horse farm, or an old barn.
★ Glam your music video up with lots of graphics and backdrops and quick cuts.

KIDZ BOP NOTES

Taylor Swift was the first country music artist to win an MTV Music Video Award. She took home the rockin' man-on-the-moon prize for the music video "You Belong with Me."

KIDZ BOP Kid Charisma's Five Fave Country Music Videos

1. "Cowboy Casanova" by Carrie Underwood
2. "The House That Built Me" by Miranda Lambert
3. "Life Is a Highway" covered by Rascal Flatts
4. "Love Story" by Taylor Swift
5. "Put You in a Song" by Keith Urban

Your KIDZ BOP Country Backup Band

Every country singer needs a band. You can strum your way to stardom solo, but it's a lot more fun with a band. You can put together your own band or you can find one and talk them into letting you sing with them. With your chops, it's a cinch! (More on this in Part Three.)

But no matter how you get the band together, you'll need to make sure that you have the musicians you need playing the right instruments to produce the sound you're looking for. This will vary according to the kind of country music you want to perform.

There's no bluegrass without a fiddle, and no honky-tonk without a steel guitar, and no country rock without drums.

Of course, you can always create your own one-of-kind sound, and make country music history!

You go, crooner!

KIDZ BOP Crooner's Ultimate Set List

You'll need a set list—a cool country mix of classic ballads, dance tunes, and guaranteed crowd-pleasers. Choose whatever suits your voice and your band, but here are some classics that will always leave your fans begging for more:

- ★ "Fifteen" by Taylor Swift
- ★ "Leave the Pieces" by The Wreckers
- ★ "I Hope You Dance" by LeAnn Womack
- ★ "Born to Fly" by Sara Evans
- ★ "This Kiss" by Faith Hill
- ★ "You're Still the One" by Shania Twain
- ★ "Not That Far Away" by Jennette McCurdy
- ★ "Cowboy, Take Me Away" by the Dixie Chicks
- ★ "Better Life" by Keith Urban
- ★ "Life Is a Highway" (covered) by Rascal Flatts

Write a Country Hit

"[COUNTRY MUSIC] JUST SPEAKS ABOUT REAL LIFE AND ABOUT TRUTH, AND IT TELLS THINGS HOW THEY REALLY ARE."

—FAITH HILL

You may never have ventured out of the big city, and you may never have even met a cowboy, but that's no reason you can't write great country songs. You do know something about love and laughter and life—even if you haven't lived that much of it yet!

Many of country's top stars started writing songs at a very early age:

★ Dolly Parton wrote her first song, "Super Dolly," at age five for her father.

★ Taylor Swift's first song was "Lucky You," which she wrote when she was ten years old after a computer repairman taught her three chords on the guitar.

★ Brad Paisley was twelve when he wrote his first song, "Born on Christmas Day." It was this song that landed Brad his first gig on *Jamboree USA*, while he was still in junior high.

So it's never too early to tune up that guitar and pick your way to a crowd-pleasing hit!

Just remember the Golden Rule of Country Music: It's all about *feeling*. Feeling bad, feeling good, feeling mad or glad or sad. In short: Write a song that makes your BFF laugh or your mom cry, and you've written a winner!

Top 10 Topics for a KIDZ BOP Country Song

1. Your first crush
2. Your first heartbreak
3. What makes you laugh and/or cry
4. Your favorite memories
5. Your hometown
6. Your family, friends, and foes
7. Your likes and dislikes
8. Your dog
9. Your country
10. Christmas

KIDZ BOP Says: Keep a Diary

"IF YOU LISTEN TO MY ALBUMS, IT'S LIKE READING MY DIARY."

—TAYLOR SWIFT

When you write a country song, you're writing about life. *Your* life. It's crazy, contradictory, but it's true: The more personal your lyrics, the more universal the appeal. You can jump-start your songwriting process by keeping a journal, in which you record not only the events of your day but also your innermost thoughts and feelings. Then, if you find yourself stuck when you sit down to write a song, you can flip through your diary for inspiration.

No worries, you can always change the names to protect the innocent—and the not-so-innocent!

Pen Your Own KIDZ BOP Country Song

"WHEN SOMETHING IS BOTHERING ME, I WRITE A SONG THAT TELLS MY FEELINGS."

—LORETTA LYNN

Time for you to write your own stuff. Fill in the blanks below, and sing your little country heart out!

There's a new _____ in town
                        noun

Lookin' _____ as can be
              adjective

My _____ starts to _____
         noun   verb

Whenever _____ is around
              proper name

Oh, _____

proper name

Oh, _____

proper name

I'm _____ **for you**

gerund

I'm _____ **and** _____

gerund   gerund

But you don't _____

verb

No matter what I do.

Oh, _____

proper name

Oh, _____

proper name

You're so _____ **to me**

adjective

You're as _____ **as a** _____

adjective   noun

Just _____ **misery.**

adjective

So go back to _____

proper noun

Leave my _____ **alone**

noun

I was _____ **and** _____

adjective   adjective

_____ on my _____ own.
        gerund   noun

Oh, _____
            proper name

Oh, _____
            proper name

I'm _____ **for you**
            gerund

I'm _____ **and** _____
            gerund   gerund

But you don't _____
                      verb

No matter what I do.

Crooner Wardrobe Checklist for Girls

Country stars today are fashion-forward and down-home at the same time. It's modern country chic—and you'll look great in it!

- ★ Jeans
- ★ T-shirts
- ★ Sequin dresses
- ★ Anything frilly
- ★ Anything with fringe
- ★ Cowboy hats
- ★ Cowboy boots

Crooner Wardrobe Checklist for Guys

For guys singing country, the trick is to look cool and manly at the same time. Like you don't spend much time thinking about what to wear—and look amazing anyway!

★ Jeans
★ T-shirts
★ Anything black
★ Anything leather
★ Anything flannel
★ Cowboy hats
★ Cowboy boots

When They Were KIDZ

> "BE DIFFERENT, STAND OUT, AND WORK YOUR BUTT OFF."
>
> —REBA McENTIRE

You're never too young to hit the road to stardom.

★ LeAnn Rimes started singing and dancing lessons as a toddler, and was competing in local talent shows by five.
★ Carrie Underwood and Josh Turner sang in their church choirs.
★ When Tom and Mike Gossin of Gloriana were six, they were already taking piano lessons.
★ Alison Krauss began violin lessons at five.
★ Taylor Swift won a national poetry contest in the fourth grade.
★ Miranda Lambert competed in her first talent contest at ten.

So take a cue from these country crooners and dust off that guitar (or piano or mandolin or banjo or fiddle), and start singing! KIDZ BOP Crooner, you're on!

KIDZ BOP KIDS ON: COUNTRY MUSIC

STEFFAN: "I love songs that tell a story—and country songs always do that! Check out Taylor Swift's song "'Tim McGraw.'"

HANNA: "The Dixie Chicks are my fave country band—they sing and play and write songs. They do it all! I wish I could play the fiddle like Martie Maguire!"

ELIJAH: "The hippest country singer is Kid Rock!"

CHARISMA: "Girl singers like my fave Taylor Swift are girly girls—just like me!"

EVA: "I'm a fashionista, so for me it's all about what Carrie Underwood, Shania Twain, and Miranda Lambert are wearing on the red carpet!"

CHAPTER 5

KIDZ BOP Dance Machine

> "I LOVE THE WHOLE WORLD OF DANCE, BECAUSE DANCING IS REALLY THE EMOTIONS THROUGH BODILY MOVEMENT."
>
> —MICHAEL JACKSON

Love to dance as much as you love to sing—or more? Then you're a dynamic dance machine, a performer whose moves are as important as your melodies. Lucky you! You bring a dancer's presence and passion to your performances, owning the stage—and the audience!

You're in good company. From Michael Jackson and Madonna to Britney Spears and Justin Bieber, the pop stars whose stars shine the brightest are those who give the people what they want: music *and* dance!

But even if you have two left feet, you can learn how to fake it until you make it. For every dancer who learned to sing—Julianne Hough—there's a singer who learned to dance—Cory Monteith. All you need is a little practice and a lot of *Dancing with the Stars* bravado and you can get your groove on with the best of them! You know that you were born to be a dance machine if you:

★ Started dancing in your crib
★ Can't sit still when there's music playing
★ Are always the first person on the dance floor
★ Dream about dancing on Broadway

- ★ Never miss an episode of *So You Think You Can Dance*
- ★ Love choreographing your own numbers
- ★ Would welcome a dance-off with Usher
- ★ Can dance with anybody—from your crush to your grandma
- ★ Are happiest when you are dancing

KIDZ BOP Kid Elijah Says: Mix It Up

There are sooo many types of dancing—and all are fun! The trick is to figure out which best suits your personal performance style. Here are five of my faves:

- ★ Freestyle
- ★ Break dancing
- ★ Moonwalk
- ★ Pop and lock
- ★ Ballroom

Dance Your Way to Stardom

"I WANTED TO DANCE. I WANTED TO SING . . . I WANTED TO BE A STAR. I WORKED REALLY HARD AND MY DREAM CAME TRUE."

—MADONNA

The most popular dance machines use dance to set their performances apart from all the rest. They know that good dancing can elevate even the simplest tunes—and transform their numbers from average to awesome!

Watch your favorite dancers, and master their best moves. When you make up your own dances, use the steps that work for you.

And don't give up! Practice makes perfect—and when it comes to dancing, practice is fun!

> "I GREW UP BEING INTO SPORTS AND I WASN'T TRAINED TO MOVE MY BODY IN THE RIGHT WAY FOR DANCING. I'M THE LAST ONE TO GET ANY MOVES CORRECT. IN REHEARSALS IT'S ALWAYS, 'OK, ONE MORE TAKE FOR ZAC.'"
>
> —ZAC EFRON

KIDZ BOP Kid Elijah's Five Fave Dancers

1. Michael Jackson
2. Ne-Yo
3. Usher
4. Beyoncé
5. Ciara

Make a Dancin' KIDZ BOP Music Video!

The music videos fans love most are the ones where dancing takes center stage. From Michael Jackson's moonwalk and Madonna's "Vogue" to Pink's "Get the Party Started" and Justin Bieber's "Baby," dancing is what makes a good music video great—every time!

Be sure to pick a venue that's both unexpected and conducive to dancing. Justin Bieber shot "Baby" in a bowling alley; Michael Jackson's "Thriller" comes to life in a graveyard. Try a parking lot or your school gym, a baseball diamond or a dance studio. Or you can simply empty out your garage and use props and curtains and backdrops to create your own stage.

KIDZ BOP Dance Machine Prop List

- ★ Chairs
- ★ Stools
- ★ Canes
- ★ Umbrellas
- ★ Hats
- ★ Gloves
- ★ Hula Hoops
- ★ Pom-poms
- ★ Stairs
- ★ Scarves
- ★ Masks
- ★ Brooms and mops
- ★ Jump ropes
- ★ Feather boas
- ★ Sunglasses
- ★ Bling

A KIDZ BOP Chorus Line

Of course, your best dance props are, well, dancers. You can recruit your own chorus line by enlisting dancers from your:

- ★ Family and friends
- ★ Local dance academies
- ★ School glee clubs
- ★ Drama clubs
- ★ Cheerleading groups
- ★ Community theater groups
- ★ Dance departments at local colleges

Movies That Make You Wanna Dance

- ★ *Mamma Mia!*
- ★ *Honey*
- ★ *Step Up*
- ★ *Dirty Dancing*
- ★ *High School Musical*
- ★ *Mad Hot Ballroom*
- ★ *Footloose*
- ★ *Grease*
- ★ *Hairspray*
- ★ *Save the Last Dance*

Your KIDZ BOP Dance Band

Every dancer needs a beat. Which means you need a band—the more percussion, the better! In fact, you can live without most every other instrument if you have to—but you gotta have drums.

We humans have been drumming as long as we've been dancing. So if you're missing rhythm, you're missing the wind beneath your wings. There are all kinds of drums, from bongos to washboards, cymbals to snares, and more. Which you use will depend on the sound you need to get your groove on. Find yourself a good drummer—or invest in a drum machine, and experiment.

Beat It!

You can also provide your own rhythm section. Anyone can play the:

- ★ Tambourine
- ★ Maracas
- ★ Triangle

★ Castanets
★ Rainsticks
★ Cowbell

KIDZ BOP NOTES: BEATBOXING

You don't need an instrument to give you a beat if you're into beatboxing. Beatboxing is making percussion sounds with your own mouth. Give it a try.

Got a Band? Make 'Em Dance!

If you're part of a band, teach your band brothers and sisters to dance! Dancing is a great way to make rehearsals more fun, and make sure your band can put on a killer performance. So add some choreography to your act. Dance moves should never take the place of great music and vocals, but you can't overstate how much good showmanship enhances a performance, either!

Practice Makes Perfect Dance Stars

"FROM THE TIME I WAS VERY LITTLE, IT WAS SOMETHING I WOULD DO ALL THE TIME, JUST SING, DANCE AND ACT."

—JENNIFER LOPEZ

Wanna get your dance on and have fun at the same time? Google "how to" dance videos on the Internet. Ask your older brother or sister or cousin to teach you some moves. Rent dance movies or watch Michael Jackson music videos on MTV.com. And check out the KIDZ BOP Dance Party! videogame, which features dance tips from KIDZ BOP performers Charisma and Elijah and great dance tunes like "Party in the USA,"

"Thriller," and "Paparazzi." You can play alone or with a friend, and by the end of the game, you'll definitely know how to bust a move!

How Inspiring! Famous (and Some Infamous!) Dances

1. The Moonwalk—Michael Jackson's most famous dance!
2. The Hip Swivel—the dance move so hot that Elvis Presley was banned from doing it on certain TV shows in the 1950s!
3. The Twist—'50s rocker Chubby Checker started a dance craze when his hit record, "The Twist," became a dance.
4. The Pogo—the dance move that's carried out just like it sounds . . . you are basically a human pogo stick. The Pogo is sort of the unofficial dance of punk rock concerts everywhere.
5. The Napoleon Dynamite—you've seen the movie, you've seen the dance, and you know it is spectacular.
6. The Thriller—yep, another Michael Jackson entry. Clearly, you can't go wrong studying pretty much any M. J. video to pick up slick dance moves, but the entire "Thriller" video is a classic, and thanks to the Michael Jackson: The Experience videogame, you can learn them all!
7. The Riverdance—sure, it's not a dance usually associated with pop and rock, which is exactly why you could put a cool hip-hop spin on it and make it a signature move!
8. Vogue—Madonna gave us the song and showed us how to do the dance in her classic music video.
9. The Cabbage Patch—another '80s classic, it started out as a dance move, but you've probably seen it more frequently as a celebratory move used by professional football players in the end zone. Either way, it's retro cool!

KIDZ BOP KIDS ON: DANCIN' WITH THE BAND

STEFFAN: "Dancing is just a natural part of performing, especially when you're singing a great upbeat song. You know . . . you don't want to just stand around during a performance."

HANNA: "Dancing actually helps me deal with nerves when I'm performing. It takes me out of my head, and I can just sing and dance and focus on a great overall performance."

EVA: "We're always dancing around, while we're recording, while we're performing . . . it's as important as singing when you're performing and trying to put on a good show."

ELIJAH: "Charisma and I had the best time working on the KIDZ BOP videogame! There was a lot of dancing, and it's really fun now to play the game and hear our voices in it."

CHARISMA: "I loved working on the videogame! I think it shows that anyone can learn to do even the coolest dance moves. And dancing is one of my favorite things about being a performer."

KIDZ BOP Dance Machine's Ultimate Set List

Here are Elijah's favorite dance tunes:

When it comes to dancing, the right music is everything. Here are some dance-friendly tunes that will get you in the mood to boogie:

- ★ "Evacuate the Dance Floor" by Cascada
- ★ "Bebot" by Black Eyed Peas
- ★ "Man in The Mirror" by Michael Jackson
- ★ "4 Minutes" by Madonna and Justin Timberlake
- ★ "Umbrella" by Rihanna
- ★ "Crazy in Love" by Beyoncé
- ★ "Telephone" by Lady Gaga featuring Beyoncé

- ★ "Magic" by B.o.B featuring Rivers Cuomo
- ★ "California Girls" by Katy Perry
- ★ "Get The Party Started" by Pink
- ★ "Thriller" by Michael Jackson
- ★ "My Love" by Justin Timberlake
- ★ "DJ Got Us Fallin' In Love" by Usher
- ★ "Pop" by 'N Sync
- ★ "1, 2 Step" by Ciara
- ★ "(Single Ladies) Put a Ring on It" by Beyoncé
- ★ "Rhythm Nation" by Janet Jackson
- ★ "When I Grow Up" by the Pussycat Dolls

KIDZ BOP Notes: Take Dance Lessons

If you want to be a great dancer, you need to dance. If you can afford professional lessons, then take them. Check out your local dance academies—but don't sign up until you ask around. Seek out the best dancers you know at school, at church, and in your neighborhood. Find out where they learned to dance—and ask for recommendations. Dance lessons can be expensive, so you want to be sure to get your money's worth!

But whether you take lessons or not, there's a lot you can teach yourself.

Try one of the Wii dance games, like Dance Dance Revolution, Just Dance, or KIDZ BOP Dance Party!—learning to dance never gets more fun than this!

Study the moves of your fave movers and shakers, and try them at home, preferably in front of a full-length mirror. Tape your dance sessions and watch yourself. And then dance some more.

Get Your Own KIDZ BOP Dance Party Started

Dancing alone is fun but dancing with your BFFs is even better! Invite your friends over for a dance party, and go crazy!

- ★ Turn your living room into a dance hall. Decorate with posters, blinking white lights, disco balls—use your imagination!
- ★ Have a playlist of all your favorite KIDZ BOP tunes—line 'em up on your CD player or iPod.
- ★ Play your favorite dancing flicks on the big screen (with the sound off) for some cool background images.
- ★ Shoot some video while you're at it.
- ★ Dress up in costumes, the more outrageous the better, to encourage the most creative dancing.
- ★ Stock up on munchies and drinks—so you can fuel up when your energy lags. And get back on the dance floor!
- ★ Now, dance till you drop!

KIDZ BOP NOTES: KEEP A VIDEO DANCE DIARY

Download your favorite dances from your favorite TV dance shows and check out the KIDZ BOP music videos on KIDZBOP.com. Collect them in a video dance diary you can turn to for inspiration whenever you need it—as well as for reference. And don't forget to add your own dance videos—because you're a dance machine, too!

Dressed to Dance

If you're a dance machine, you need clothes that move with you—and still look great. Practically anything goes—from the traditional dancer's uniform of tights and tutus to baggy jeans and oversized T-shirts. The trick is to use fabrics with some stretch in them, so nothing you're wearing restricts you in any way.

Plan your accessories with your moves in mind, too—you don't want to whack yourself in the head with baubles, bangles, and beads!

KIDZ BOP Dance Machine Wardrobe Checklist for Girls

You can dance your way to glam in:

★ Jeans
★ Tights or leggings
★ Short skirts or shorts
★ Sequin dresses
★ Fun jewelry
★ Anything animal print
★ Sparkly shirts
★ Ballet slippers
★ Shiny flats
★ Brightly colored sneakers
★ Boots

KIDZ BOP Dance Machine Wardrobe Checklist for Guys

Guys who dance are cool without even trying. You can wear whatever you want—as long as you can move in it.

★ Baggy jeans—or not
★ T-shirts
★ Caps
★ Anything black
★ Retro patterns
★ Sneakers
★ Boots

When They Were KIDZ

"IT'S NOT JUST DANCE MOVES . . . IT'S ENTERTAINMENT. PERIOD."

—USHER

The performers who qualify as Dance Machines loved to dance from an early age:

★ When *Glee*'s Harry Shum, Jr., was in high school, he tried out for the dance team on a dare—and the rest is *Glee* history.
★ By the time he was twelve, Justin Bieber was posting videos of his performances on YouTube.
★ At thirteen, Usher appeared on *Star Search*.
★ When Justin Timberlake was twelve, he was dancing on *The Mickey Mouse Club* with Britney Spears.
★ At eight, Michael Jackson was singing and dancing with his brothers in the Jackson 5.
★ Paula Abdul took ballet, tap, and jazz lessons as a child.

Usher, the ultimate dance machine himself, gets it right when he says that dancing is all about entertainment. So put on your dancing shoes, and give your performances the awesome moves they need to rock the house!

KIDZ BOP KIDS ON: MY DREAM DANCE PARTNER

STEFFAN: "You mean I'd have to choose between Fergie and Lady Gaga?"

HANNA: "That's easy—Justin Bieber. He's so cute—and he knows how to dance!"

ELIJAH: "Beyoncé! Beyoncé! Beyoncé!"

CHARISMA: "In my dreams, I'd host a sleepover and invite Miley Cyrus, Britney Spears, Julianne Hough, and *Glee*'s Heather Morris and Jenna Ushkowitz—and we'd dance all night!"

EVA: "I'd go Charisma one further—and put on a dance party in the school gym and invite all the professional dancers on *Dancing with the Stars* to teach me and my classmates all the coolest moves!"

CHAPTER 6

KIDZ BOP Hip-Hop/R&B Pop Star

> "WHEN I GET ONSTAGE I GIVE 100 PERCENT AND I ONLY HOPE THAT MY FANS WILL ENJOY WHAT I PUT TOGETHER."
>
> —USHER

> "IN MY MIND I HAVE ALWAYS BEEN AN A-LIST HOLLYWOOD SUPERSTAR. Y'ALL JUST DIDN'T KNOW IT YET."
>
> —WILL SMITH

If you love Usher—and who doesn't?—then you know that some of the biggest names in music start out singing R&B, hip-hop, rap, or some combination of the these popular kinds of music.

You know that you were born to be a hip-hopper if you:

★ Think rhyming is as easy as talking
★ Have a highly refined sense of rhythm
★ Are the coolest dresser you know
★ Think the dream concert would be Ciara and Jay-Z and Kanye West
★ Have a voice that could melt butter

★ Love to improvise and freestyle
★ Have something to say—and need to say it

Whether you'd rather groove to the mellow soul of pure R&B or rock out with rappers and hip-hoppers, the good news is: It's all fun!

Write a KIDZ BOP Hip-Hop/R&B Hit

> "I LOVE MY OWN MUSIC. IF I DIDN'T LOVE IT, I WOULDN'T RECORD IT . . . [MY MUSIC] IS ALWAYS ME AND IT'S ALWAYS THE TRUTH."
>
> —ALICIA KEYS

Writing a great hip-hop song requires the perfect combination of exceptional:

★ Concept or story
★ Rhyming wordplay
★ Beat selection

If you're trying your hand at pure R&B songwriting, you'll need a little less rhyme—and a lot more soul. But the biggest hits often combine both hip-hop elements and R&B.

Make your song be about something that means something to you. You don't have to be a rebel to write something that says something—but if you are, all the better!

Top 10 Topics for a KIDZ BOP Hip-Hop/R&B Song

1. Growing up
2. Trying to fit in
3. Hanging out

4. Falling in love
5. Breaking up
6. Secret crush
7. Cliques
8. Girl power
9. Guy power
10. Stardom

Pen Your Own KIDZ BOP Hip-Hop/R&B Song

> "IT'S ABOUT HOW REAL ARE YOU, OR HOW STRONG CAN YOU BE, AND REALLY MY MUSIC JUST REFLECTS ME. IF YOU CAN ACCEPT ME, THEN YOU CAN ACCEPT MY MUSIC."
>
> —NICK CANNON

Time for you to write a song that gets all your friends moving and grooving and rhyming. Use one of the writing prompts below to jump-start your songwriting:

★ When I met you for the first time . . .
★ I love being a girl because . . .
★ That girl is a mean girl—but that doesn't mean I . . .
★ Sshhh! Don't reveal my secret crush . . .
★ I used to miss you, but now . . .
★ When I'm a big star, I going to . . .
★ If I could change one thing, I'd . . .

KIDZ BOP Hip-Hop/R&B Ultimate Set List

- ★ "Heartless" by Kanye West
- ★ "Whip Your Hair" by Willow Smith
- ★ "Boom Boom Pow" by the Black Eyed Peas
- ★ "Empire State of Mind" covered by the cast of *Glee*
- ★ "Break Your Heart" by Taio Cruz
- ★ "Ladies First" by Queen Latifah
- ★ "Airplanes" by B.o.B featuring Hayley Williams
- ★ "1, 2 Step" by Ciara
- ★ "Fire Burning" by Sean Kingston
- ★ "Men in Black" by Will Smith

Make a Hip-Hop/R&B KIDZ BOP Music Video!

"THE BEAUTIFUL THING ABOUT HIP-HOP IS IT'S LIKE AN AUDIO COLLAGE. YOU CAN TAKE ANY FORM OF MUSIC AND DO IT IN A HIP-HOP WAY AND IT'LL BE A HIP-HOP SONG. THAT'S THE ONLY MUSIC YOU CAN DO THAT WITH."

—TALIB KWELI

Talib Kweli is right—so do what the biggest names in the music business do and combine the soul of R&B with the beat of hip-hop. It's the fastest way to the top of the charts!

You can set your video anywhere, but the most traditional settings are:

- ★ On the street
- ★ Parking lots
- ★ Clubs
- ★ Warehouses

★ Malls
★ Parking garages

Elijah's Top Hip-Hop/R&B Music Covered by KIDZ BOP

★ "Airplanes" by B.o.B. featuring Hayley Williams
★ "Heartless" by Kanye West
★ "Just a Dream" by Nelly
★ "No One" by Alicia Keys
★ "Beautiful Girls" by Sean Kingston
★ "1, 2 Step" by Ciara
★ "Burn" by Usher
★ "Let's Get It Started" by Black Eyed Peas

KIDZ BOP Hip-Hop/R&B Wardrobe Checklist for Girls

You can rap and break dance your way to glam in:

★ Tight jeans with—or without—shreds
★ T-shirts with cartoon characters or messages on them
★ Short skirts
★ Laddered stockings
★ One-shouldered tops and dresses
★ Knitted sweaters and scarves
★ Bling
★ Sneakers
★ Open-toed boots
★ High heels

KIDZ BOP Hip-Hop/R&B Wardrobe Checklist for Guys

Hip-hoppers and R&B artists get away with clothes that your average guy could never pull off, including:

- ★ Baggy jeans—or tight jeans
- ★ Low pants
- ★ T-shirts with cartoon characters or messages on them
- ★ Black leather jackets
- ★ Sunglasses
- ★ Bling
- ★ Knitted caps
- ★ Hats (tipped to the side)
- ★ Striped shirts
- ★ Athletic jerseys
- ★ Track suits
- ★ Sneakers
- ★ Boots
- ★ Hoodies

When They Were KIDZ

- ★ Usher started singing in the church choir when he was only six.
- ★ Jay-Z used the kitchen table as a drumming surface when he was little.
- ★ In high school, Queen Latifah formed the girl rapper group Ladies Fresh with BFFs Tangy B and Landy D.
- ★ Joseph "Run" Simmons of Run DMC started DJing and beatboxing as a teenager in Queens.

KIDZ BOP KIDS ON: FAVE HIP-HOP/R&B ARTISTS

STEFFAN: "Usher is the coolest guy in show business. He sings great and he looks great. When I'm a big star, I'm going to dress just like he does."

EVA: "I just love Willow Smith. 'Whip Your Hair' is awesome!"

ELIJAH: "Beyoncé and Jay-Z are the perfect musical couple. I love their duets, especially 'Crazy in Love.'"

CHARISMA: "Alicia Keys is such a great songwriter. I'd like to play the piano and write songs like that. I'm working on it!"

HANNA: "Ever since I was a little girl, I've loved Queen Latifah. She can do anything—from rap to Broadway."

CHAPTER 7

KIDZ BOP Showstopper

> "I AM FOCUSED ON THE WORK. I AM CONSTANTLY CREATING. I AM A BUSY GIRL. I LIVE AND BREATHE MY WORK. I LOVE WHAT I DO. I BELIEVE IN THE MESSAGE. THERE'S NO STOPPING. I DIDN'T CREATE THE FAME, THE FAME CREATED ME."
>
> —LADY GAGA

There are some performers who walk out onstage and suddenly everyone else just disappears from view. These are the showstoppers, the Beyoncés and Mariahs and Gagas of the world!

You, too, can be a showstopper. It's not a question of talent—although you've got to have talent. It's a presence, a persona, a passion that sets you apart, high above all the rest. You have to be You with a capital *Y*!

You know that you were born to be a showstopper if you:

★ Are usually the center of attention
★ Leave adoring fans in your wake wherever you go
★ Practice signing your name for autographs
★ Have more energy than anyone else you know
★ Make it a point to make an impression on everyone you meet
★ Think the perfect triple-threat concert would be Me, Myself, and I!
★ Would never leave the house without looking your best
★ Have a signature style as big as your personality

★ Work hard to make your performances look effortless

★ Know what it takes to grab the spotlight—and keep it

Bringing the House Down

If you're a showstopper, you want only one thing: Bring the house down! No matter where you are or who you're with, you want the audience to remember you, and you alone.

To pull off that magic diva trick, you need to work harder—and smarter—than everybody else. You need to deliver a polished performance that sets you apart.

KIDZ BOP SAYS: 7 SECRETS OF SHOWSTOPPERS!

You want to capture your audience's attention—and hold it as long as you need to. Which is basically whenever you're onstage!

When you're a showstopper, you step onstage, and everybody's eyes are on you. Nobody talks, nobody fidgets, nobody gets up to go to the bathroom. You cast a spell on the audience—and they are caught up in your magic.

But how you do that? Here are the KIDZ BOP 7 Secrets of Showstoppers:

1. Charm your audience. You want your audience not only to like you, but to *love* you!
2. Move like you're a star. This is not so much great dancing as attitude. Make your audience believe that you were born under a spotlight!
3. Milk your charisma. Personality is as much a part of being a showstopper as your performance.
4. Rehearse till you can rock it in your sleep. When you're onstage, you can't be thinking about what notes to sing or which moves to

make. You have to have all that down so you can focus on your audience.

5. Relate to your fans. Sure, you want them to think you're a goddess, but you also want them to think you're one of them. No one likes a conceited goddess!

6. Be ready for anything. Anything can happen when you're performing—and you've got to roll with it. Even mistakes become opportunities to impress your audience with your quick-witted talent!

7. Think big, bigger, biggest! There's nothing subtle about a showstopper. Everything about your performance—from the song you sing to the clothes you wear—needs to generate excitement! When in doubt, go bigger!

KIDZ BOP Notes: Know Your Competition!

Being the star who dominates the stage means beating out all the other people onstage. So being a showstopper requires a healthy love of competition. Showstoppers study their peers, their betters, and their mentors, not only to improve their own performances, but to beat their competition at their own game.

You should do the same!

> "DIANA ROSS IS A BIG INSPIRATION TO ALL OF US. WE ALL GREW UP WATCHING EVERYTHING ABOUT HER—HER MIKE PLACEMENT, HER GRACE, HER STYLE AND HER CLASS."
>
> —BEYONCÉ

There's only one place for a showstopper to go to study the art of diva—other divas! Here's a list of the diva-licious pop stars you should study.

Top Showstoppers of All Time

1. Diana Ross
2. Barbra Streisand
3. Tina Turner
4. Bette Midler
5. Celine Dion
6. Beyoncé
7. Whitney Houston
8. Mariah Carey
9. Christina Aguilera
10. Lady Gaga
11. Janet Jackson
12. Jennifer Hudson

Make a Rockin' KIDZ BOP Showstopper Video!

If you're a showstopper, you know that you must do whatever it takes to blow your fans away—one frame at a time!

★ Start with an awesome song that's worthy of you and your ambition.

★ Add the very best choreography—enlist the help of the best dancers you know if this is not one of your strengths.

★ Where you set your video doesn't matter as long as you stage your number as an extravaganza. Showstopping performances are over the top—so make yours over the top as well. This means great backdrops and props and more.

★ Costumes are everything—so go wild. And not just for you, but for your backup singers and dancers as well.

★ Showstoppers are drama queens—in the best sense of the word. So make a dramatic music video!

Here are KIDZ BOP Kid Hanna's five fave showstopper music videos:

1. "Telephone" by Lady Gaga
2. "I'm a Good Girl" by Christina Aguilera
3. "Sweet Dreams" by Beyoncé
4. "Waiting for Tonight" by Jennifer Lopez
5. "Rhythm Nation" by Janet Jackson

Your KIDZ BOP Showstopper Backup Band

Being a showstopper means that you have the tools to wow 'em every time. So whether you're fronting a band or singing a solo with the church choir or competing in a local talent show, you need to know you're getting the backup you need.

The trick is to share your vision of the performance—paint an irresistible picture!—and emphasize their role in executing that vision. They can bask in your reflected glory—as you take the place by storm!

KIDZ BOP Showstopper's Ultimate Set List

The perfect pop princess set list is one that spotlights your unique gifts *and* draws a crowd. Here are some classics that are guaranteed to keep the spotlight on you!

★ "If I Were a Boy" by Beyoncé
★ "Hero" by Mariah Carey
★ "I Will Always Love You" by Whitney Houston
★ "Telephone" by Lady Gaga
★ "Together Again" by Janet Jackson
★ "My Heart Will Go On" by Celine Dion
★ "Beautiful" by Christina Aguilera

Write a Showstopper Hit

You can't be a showstopper without great songs to sing even if you have to write them yourself.

After all, all of today's great showstoppers write their own songs. Most started writing them early on in their career, because they knew that every great performance starts with a great song.

So you need to write your own songs if you want to be a showstopper. And these songs need to be as big as your talent. No modest little love songs; we're talking dramatic songs with attitude!

Top 10 Topics for a KIDZ BOP Showstopper Song

1. Where is the love of your life
2. The kiss that changed everything
3. Why he dumped you
4. Why you dumped him
5. Dance, dance, dance
6. Mean girls
7. BFFs forever
8. Girl power
9. Issue song (in which you promote your favorite cause)
10. Tribute song (in which you honor your favorite hero)

Pen Your Own KIDZ BOP Showstopper Song

Remember, it's all about drama! So think drama queen when you write a song using one of the following prompts:

★ When you broke my heart, I thought I'd . . .
★ When the world gets tough, I . . .
★ What I love about summer is . . .

★ I'm so done with you, so it's your turn to . . .
★ If it's Saturday night, I'm dancing with . . .
★ You are my hero because . . .

Showstopper Wardrobe Checklist

There's no such thing as a typical showstopper wardrobe. If you're a showstopper, you don't wear clothes, you wear costumes!

★ Jeans
★ T-shirts
★ Dresses, skirts, jumpsuits
★ Animal prints, geometric prints
★ Anything that sparkles, shines, or glitters
★ Extreme accessories
★ Big jewelry that you can't miss
★ Wigs and/or hair extensions
★ Shoes that let you glide onto the stage

KIDZ BOP Showstopper Style Guide: Fashion to the Max!

> "AND NOW, I'M JUST TRYING TO CHANGE THE WORLD, ONE SEQUIN AT A TIME."
>
> —LADY GAGA

Showstoppers always make a fashion statement—whether they're at the grocery store or strutting down the red carpet. Lady Gaga and Katy Perry are two showstoppers whose unique—some may say just plain weird—outfits always stop the show!

When They Were KIDZ

> "BASICALLY, I STARTED SINGING WHEN I STARTED TALKING. MUSIC HAS JUST BEEN MY SAVING GRACE MY WHOLE LIFE."
>
> —MARIAH CAREY

Showstoppers learn the importance of making a mark early:

★ Mariah Carey worked as a demo singer when she was still in high school.

★ Beyoncé was in her first group, Girl's Tyme, at the age of eight.

★ As a little girl Celine Dion sang with her brothers and sisters at her mom and dad's piano bar.

★ Lady Gaga began playing the piano at four—and writing songs at thirteen.

★ Jennifer Hudson started singing in the church choir at seven.

★ By seven, Janet Jackson was performing with the Jackson 5 in Las Vegas.

★ When Christina Aguilera was a child, the local press dubbed her "the little girl with the big voice."

If you're a showstopper, it's time to turn on the applause meter and raise the curtain on your talent . . . starting now!

KIDZ BOP KIDS ON: FAVE SHOWSTOPPERS

STEFFAN: "Christina Aguilera stops the show for me every time I hear her sing 'You Lost Me'!"

HANNA: "Katy Perry is my fave performer. She's fun and funky and always true to herself!"

ELIJAH: "For me, it's always Beyoncé. She has so much energy onstage—and gives her all every time."

EVA: "My parents took me to a Madonna concert when I was in grade school and I'll never forget it. She can really put on a show! I knew then I wanted to do the same thing someday!"

CHARISMA: "My mom loves Cher, and ever since I was little we've danced around the house together listening to her songs. So she was my first showstopper!"

CHAPTER 8
KIDZ BOP 360 Degrees

"I'M A PERFECTIONIST. I CAN'T HELP IT; I GET REALLY UPSET WITH MYSELF IF I FAIL IN THE LEAST."

—JUSTIN TIMBERLAKE

If you can do it all—act, sing, dance—then you're one of the chosen few who are the rarest performers on earth: the 360s!

The 360s blow everyone else away in terms of versatility and talent, moving from TV and film to concert tours to Broadway with an explosive ease the rest of us can only sit back and admire.

But there's something else just as important that sets a 360 apart: perfectionism and hard work. If you're a 360, you can leverage these qualities all the way to the top!

You know that you were born to be a 360 if you:

★ Work harder and longer than anyone else
★ Enjoy acting and dancing as much as you love singing
★ Seek out mentors and teachers who can help you get to the next level
★ Push everyone you perform with to do their very best
★ Have very high expectations—and strive to meet them
★ Always give 150 percent—because 100 percent just isn't good enough

It's All about the Work

> "AS SOON AS I STEP ON THAT STAGE, NOTHING MATTERS. I DON'T THINK OF IT AS WORK. IT'S JUST SO MUCH FUN."
>
> —MILEY CYRUS

If you're a 360, you work hard—but you don't think of it as work. You love what you do, and live and breathe your work. There's nothing you'd rather be doing, and when you're not doing it, you're thinking about doing it.

More to the point, you're thinking about doing it *better*.

Doing It All—and Lovin' It!

When you're a 360, you love doing it all. You couldn't choose between dancing and singing and acting—even if you had to!

The good news is you don't have to!

Your biggest problem is how to fit it all in—in only twenty-four hours a day!

KIDZ BOP KIDS ON: THE 360 PLAN

STEFFAN: "Never say never. Whenever I find myself thinking, 'I could never do that,' I stop myself and remember all the things I used to think I couldn't do that I do now all the time. Like being a KIDZ BOP Kid!"

ELIJAH: "I try to learn from the best teachers. I know how lucky I am to be able to take voice lessons and dancing lessons and acting lessons—so I work hard!"

EVA: "I audition for everything—and why not? You never know what you can do until you try. That's how I got my first gig—for a local pizza restaurant!"

CHARISMA: "I'm in a band back home and they made me the leader because I like to organize everything. I keep everybody on track when rehearsals run long or the music isn't coming together like it should. And I never forget to bring the snacks!"

HANNA: "I can get so focused on rehearsing and performing that I forget to get a life. My mom helps remind me that you still need to take time for just hanging out with your family and friends."

> "AS AN ACTRESS, AND AS A PERSON, I HAVE ALWAYS LIKED TO CHALLENGE MYSELF."
>
> —ASHLEY TISDALE

And the Triple-Threat Winner Is . . .

> "AT WORK, WE HAVE A NICKNAME FOR MATT MORRISON—WE CALL HIM 'TRIPLE THREAT,' BECAUSE HE'S AN INCREDIBLE SINGER-DANCER-ACTOR. AND NOW I GET TO BORROW THAT PHRASE, WHICH IS REALLY COOL."
>
> —LEA MICHELE

But it was Broadway star and *Glee* songbird Lea Michele herself who was the first performer ever awarded *Billboard*'s Triple Threat Award. Apparently, at *Glee* the triple threat is catching!

Make a Rockin' KIDZ BOP 360 Video!

> "... A video like 'Cry Me a River' [was] kind of a short film. Then I worked on another video for a song I wrote called 'What Goes Around,' [which was also in] a short film style. I find it much easier to tell a narrative—you have four minutes, you can kind of jump through things—but [it's] very similar to making a short film."
>
> —Justin Timberlake

When a 360 makes a music video, it's not a music video, it's an event! These are the music videos that tell a story, break the mold, set a new bar of excellence.

★ If you're a 360, you want to make a video that showcases all of your talents—and will leave your audience begging for more!

★ Start with a story idea—and then build the music video around that.

★ Write/choose a great song that suits your story idea.

★ Choreography should help tell the story you want to tell—from beginning to end.

★ Cast your video with the best dancers and singers you can, so you don't have to tell the story all by yourself.

★ Choose the setting that best dramatizes the story—be it your backyard or your local tourist attraction.

★ Everyone in your video is a character in your story—so costume each character accordingly.

★ The 360 video is a mini-musical—so think big and go for broke!

360 Videos to Check Out

★ "Cry Me a River" by Justin Timberlake
★ "Clumsy" by Fergie

★ "These Boots Are Made for Walkin'" by Jessica Simpson
★ "Start All Over" by Miley Cyrus
★ "It's Alright, It's Okay" by Ashley Tisdale
★ "4 Minutes" by Justin Timberlake and Madonna

Your KIDZ BOP 360 Band

When you're a 360, you don't believe in "backup" bands. There's nothing "backup" about your collaborators. You know that you need your fellow musicians—and dancers and designers and actors, for that matter—to make the performance the best it can be, which is all you really care about. Try performing with all kinds of bands, like:

★ School marching bands
★ Garage bands
★ Symphony orchestras
★ String quartets
★ Rock bands
★ Jazz musicians
★ Street musicians
★ Church choirs

KIDZ BOP SAYS: COLLABORATE!

If you're a 360, you love working with talented people because it fuels your creative process. And for you, that's what it's all about. So seek out collaborators for every aspect of your work—from songwriting and choreography to staging, scripting, and directing. You'll be glad you did!

Write a 360 Hit

"I WRITE ALL THE TIME. I WAS WRITING SONGS LAST NIGHT.... I SHOULDN'T HAVE STAYED UP UNTIL 2 IN THE MORNING WRITING SONGS! BUT YOU JUST GET SO INTO IT THAT YOU CAN'T STOP."

—MILEY CYRUS

If you're a 360, then odds are you're a songwriter as well as a singer, dancer, and actor. You like to try your hand at everything—and you don't give up until you get it right. Many of our most successful 360s—Justin Timberlake, Miley Cyrus, Fergie, among others—write their own songs, as well as songs for other people.

If you're writing songs, you want to follow their example, and write tunes that can carry the most exciting performances.

Top 10 Topics for a KIDZ BOP 360 Story Song

1. Your first love
2. The girl/guy who got away
3. Revenge
4. Saturday night
5. Dancing to forget her/him
6. Facing down your enemy
7. Saving someone's life
8. Getting your girl/guy back
9. What keeps you up at night
10. Road trip

Pen Your Own KIDZ BOP 360 Song

Remember: You want to write a song that you can easily script and stage into a showcase that allows your singing, dancing, and acting talents to shine!

Here's a brainstorming exercise to help you come up with great song ideas that are right for your talent.

Sit down with a pen and paper and write the first thing that pops into your mind when you think about:

★ Your favorite dance. Is it fast, slow, upbeat? What style dance is it?

★ Your favorite song. Is it happy, sad, danceable?

★ Your favorite KIDZ BOP videos. Why do you like them? What's special about the way they are done?

★ Your favorite TV dance shows. What are your favorite numbers? Why?

★ Your favorite musicals. What parts do you like best? Why?

360 Wardrobe Checklist

"I HELPED PUT TOGETHER SHARPAY'S LOOK, AND I WANTED IT TO BE OVER-THE-TOP, FLASHY, ATTENTION-GETTING, BECAUSE THAT'S HER. BUT SHE HAS A HEART. YOU NEVER KNOW WHAT SOMEONE IS ABOUT."

—ASHLEY TISDALE

"EVERYONE HAS THEIR DIFFERENT LOOK. . . . WILL'S GOT HIS KNICKERS AND CRAZY SOCKS, AND TABOO HAS HIS KUNG FU WEAR. I HAVE TO THINK OF WORDS TO PUT MY STYLE INTO. I WOULD SAY KIND OF URBAN GYPSY, BECAUSE I COLLECT THINGS, ACCESSORIES, FROM ALL OVER THE WORLD [ASIA, AFRICA, BRAZIL], AND THAT IS DEFINITELY WHAT, FOR ME, HELPS MAKE AN OUTFIT MY OWN."

—FERGIE

If you're a 360, you have two separate performance wardrobes:

Your personal performance wardrobe.
The clothes you wear onstage when you are just singing—not putting on a number—are simply a grander version of what you wear in your personal life. You'll have your own style; you know who you are, and your wardrobe reflects that.

Your role performance wardrobe.
When you're part of an act, whether you're singing and dancing in a musical number or acting in a play or TV show or film, you are in character—and what you wear is what your character would wear. You take care to wear the right clothes for the role—because you know that those clothes help you get into character—and stay in character!

When They Were KIDZ

> "[WHEN I WAS YOUNG] I'D GO TO CONCERTS AND THINK, 'THAT'S EXACTLY WHAT I WANT TO DO.'"
>
> —JESSICA SIMPSON

360s are obsessed with performing from an early age:

★ Miley Cyrus decided she wanted to go into show business when she was eight after seeing a production of *Mamma Mia!*.

★ Matthew Morrison decided to become a performer after going to theater camp as a kid.

★ Lea Michele won her first Broadway role at the age of eight.

★ Fergie took dance lessons as a child—and by nine was cast in *Kids Incorporated.*

★ Ashley Tisdale was discovered at a New Jersey mall at three.

★ Neil Patrick Harris was discovered at a New Mexico drama camp he attended as a child.

★ Jessica Simpson started singing as a kid in the choir at the local Baptist church.

★ As a kid, Justin Timberlake appeared on *The New Mickey Mouse Club* with fellow cast members Britney Spears and Christina Aguilera.

If you're a 360, you know that life's one long performance—so start rehearsing today!

KIDZ BOP KIDS ON: 360 SUPERSTARS

STEFFAN: "Justin Timberlake is so talented—and he keeps on trying new things. I'm modeling my career in show business after him!"

ELIJAH: "I'd like to have a career like Will Smith's—which I think I can do, since I already dance better than he does!"

HANNA: "I love being part of KIDZ BOP—and I love performing solo. So I'd choose Fergie, because she's part of the Black Eyed Peas, but she also does her own thing."

EVA: "Jessica Simpson not only sings and dances and acts, she also has her own line of shoes—now that's what I want to do!"

CHARISMA: "*Hannah Montana* is my favorite TV show of all time. Miley Cyrus played that double role so perfectly—just like a true 360!"

PART THREE

CHAPTER 9
Band on the Rise

> "As GOOD AS I AM, I'M NOTHING WITHOUT MY BAND."
>
> —STEVEN TYLER OF AEROSMITH

The good news: Being in a band can be the best experience of your music career. You can work closely with other talented people, you can meet new people who may become lifelong friends, and you can strengthen your own talents by surrounding yourself with others who take their craft as seriously as you do. Oh, and you can have a lot of fun!

As with all other aspects of forging a career in the music industry, being in a band is also a lot of hard work. On the one hand, you get to share everything, good and bad. On the other hand, it's not all about you, about what you want, about what is best for your career. There can be personality clashes, conflicts of interest in terms of what direction the band will go, fights about some members not pulling their weight. . . . Bottom line: Sometimes, a band just doesn't work, and it's not anyone's fault. It's like any other relationship in life; sometimes people just aren't compatible enough to be bandmates.

We'll dish more on that later in this section, specifically ways to ensure your band stays together. But for now, let's delve into the different types of bands you might create!

Why be in a band, instead of pursuing a solo career? Let us count the reasons why. . . .

Even Superstars Need Backup

1. You don't have to do it alone. You share the work, you share the responsibilities, you share the glory!
2. It's fun!
3. You don't have to master everything. You can be a singer or a songwriter or play an instrument or a combination of those roles, but you don't have to do all three (not to mention dance, choreograph performances, or handle the business side of performing) all by yourself.
4. The chance to form lifelong bonds with people who share the same passions you do.
5. Being around other talented people will only serve to strengthen your own talents.
6. The chance to learn to get along with other people, including some who may be difficult.
7. The chance to learn serious organization skills; being in a band is the ultimate exercise in project management.
8. When you're starting your career, it can be easier to get paying gigs as a band. . . . Customers think they're getting a whole group for one price (and they're right!).
9. Bands sometimes produce more creative work, because you have several people bringing ideas and talent into the mix.
10. Being part of a group can give you the confidence to be freer with your performances, to take more chances, which can lead to great things for the whole band.

More Than the Sum of Its Parts

You've heard the saying "The whole is greater than the sum of its parts"? In this case, it would mean that a band's potential is better than the potential for all of its members individually. But don't take our word for it. . . . Here's what the KIDZ BOP Kids have to say about band-ing together!

KIDZ BOP KIDS ON: ROCKIN' TOGETHER

STEFFAN: "I know I wouldn't be having as much fun as a performer if I wasn't a member of a group. There are so many fun things about this job, and I'm excited that I have good friends who are right there experiencing them with me."

HANNA: "I love being in the spotlight, and singing solos, but it's hard for me to imagine doing that all the time. I love the KIDZ BOP Kids, and we really are like our own little family."

EVA: "The best thing about being in a band is that I know there are always at least four other people who know exactly what I'm feeling, how hard I'm working. There are times when we miss our friends or family, or we miss out on some school thing because we're working, but it's happening to all of us, and we are all there to support each other in those times, and celebrate together in the good times."

ELIJAH: "This is the most fun thing I've done in my life, and I know it would be way less fun without the other KIDZ BOP Kids."

CHARISMA: "I love the fact that I get to work with other kids who have the same big goals as me, but who are also different in a lot of ways, and that's awesome! I like that we all have our own strengths and special skills, because it makes us all better singers, better performers, better dancers, and better people. I love our group!"

Backup Singers

You could get your start in music as a backup singer. A backup singer provides vocal harmony with the lead vocalist or other backing vocalists.

As a backup singer, you'll:

★ Sing a lead-in at the beginning of the song
★ Harmonize with the lead vocalist
★ Sing a countermelody to what the lead vocalist is singing
★ You could be hired solely for recording sessions, but most often, you'll back up the lead vocalist in live performances

KIDZ BOP Notes: Backup, Anyone?

In many rock bands, the musicians also sing backup, and in some groups backup singers also dance. And some lead vocalists do their own backups in the recording studio.

Backup singers in rock bands:

★ Beach Boys (Carl Wilson, Al Jardine, Dennis Wilson)
★ The Beatles (George Harrison and Ringo Starr)
★ The Rolling Stones (Keith Richards)
★ Red Hot Chili Peppers (John Frusciante)
★ Bon Jovi (Richie Sambora, David Bryan, and Hugh McDonald)
★ Fall Out Boy (Pete Wentz and Joe Trohman)
★ Paramore (Josh Farro)
★ My Chemical Romance (Ray Toro and Frank Leno)

Lead singers who like to record their own backup vocals:

★ David Bowie
★ Freddie Mercury of Queen
★ Steven Tyler of Aerosmith
★ Robert Smith of the Cure

- ★ Mariah Carey
- ★ Michael Jackson
- ★ Janet Jackson
- ★ Beyoncé Knowles
- ★ Brandy
- ★ Faith Evans
- ★ D'Angelo
- ★ Amerie

Backup singers who went on to become huge stars in their own right:

- ★ Elton John
- ★ Cher
- ★ Phil Collins
- ★ Whitney Houston
- ★ Dave Grohl
- ★ Sheryl Crow
- ★ Mariah Carey
- ★ Gwen Stefani
- ★ Pink

Jennifer Lopez began her career as a Fly Girl, one of the hot female dancers on the TV show *In Living Color*, which was a huge hit in the early 1990s. She made a brief cameo appearance in a Janet Jackson video and soon thereafter launched her own singing career.

KIDZ BOP Kids: We Are Family

Do you have sisters or brothers or cousins who are also musically inclined? Ever thought about making music a family affair?

Singing Siblings

"WE ARE A STRONGER BAND THAN WE HAVE EVER BEEN. WE STILL MAKE MUSIC FOR THE SAME REASONS WE STARTED."

—HANSON

You've already mastered how to get along (and fight) as brothers and sisters, so who better to form a band than you and your sibs? There are tons of famous family acts who've hit the big time, and yours could be among the names on the list of our favorite singing sibling acts!

Faves . . .

1. The Jonas Brothers
2. Dixie Chicks
3. The Jackson 5
4. Hanson
5. Kings of Leon
6. Bee Gees
7. The Osmonds
8. Gladys Knight and the Pips
9. The Pointer Sisters

Tune Time: Songs You Should Know by Family Acts

★ "Burning Up" by the Jonas Brothers
★ "Cowboy Take Me Away" by the Dixie Chicks
★ "I'll Be There" by the Jackson 5

- ★ "MMMBop" by Hanson
- ★ "Stayin' Alive" by the Bee Gees
- ★ "One Bad Apple" by the Osmonds
- ★ "Midnight Train to Georgia" by Gladys Knight and the Pips
- ★ "We Are Family" by Sly and the Family Stone

KIDZ BOP Kids: Boy Band

"ONE OF OUR GREATEST PROFESSIONAL CHALLENGES IS TO BE SUCCESSFUL EVERY TIME OUT. THERE AREN'T A LOT OF ARTISTS THAT CAN BE SUCCESSFUL ALL OF THE TIME SO WE TRY TO BE OUR BEST AND DO THE BEST THAT WE CAN DO. IT'S A VERY BIG CHALLENGE FOR US."

—BOYZ II MEN

Got a group of guy friends you want to start a band with? A boy band could be the way to go. Boy bands, typically, have been comprised of members with great vocal and dance skills, but who don't necessarily play instruments. That means it's all about putting on a great performance with catchy tunes and choreography. . . . Are you up for that?

Hangin' with the Guys

The number one reason to start a boy band? Probably depends on who you ask. Or maybe it doesn't. . . . We're gonna say most members of the bands would say that it makes it pretty easy to get dates. But there's also the camaraderie of hangin' with guys who have the same musical goals you do, the chance to travel (all around the world, potentially), and, of course, the chance to make some really great tunes!

Faves . . .

1. Backstreet Boys
2. 'N Sync
3. Big Time Rush
4. New Kids on the Block
5. 98 Degrees
6. New Edition
7. The Monkees
8. Boyz II Men
9. Take That

KIDZ BOP Boy Band Hits

Here are some of Elijah's faves:

★ "I Want It That Way" by the Backstreet Boys
★ "It's Gonna Be Me" by 'N Sync
★ "Halfway There" by Big Time Rush
★ "Step by Step" by New Kids on the Block
★ "The Hardest Thing" by 98 Degrees
★ "Daydream Believer" by the Monkees
★ "End of the Road" by Boyz II Men

KIDZ BOP Kids: Girl Group

"WE DON'T TAKE OURSELVES TOO SERIOUSLY. I DON'T THINK WE'RE TRYING TO BE ANYTHING THAT WE'RE NOT. WE'RE NOT, LIKE, TRYING TO REINVENT THE WHEEL OR ANYTHING."

—NICOLE SCHERZINGER OF THE PUSSYCAT DOLLS

Anything boys can do, girls can do, too! Forming a girl group comes with all the same advantages of forming a boy band—plus, you've got all that girl power behind you!

KIDZ BOP Spotlight: Spice It Up!

"BEING IN THE SPICE GIRLS WAS AN INSANE EXPERIENCE."

—MEL C

In 1996, with the release of their record, "Wannabe," the Spice Girls became a global sensation and went on to become one of the most commercially successful British groups since the Beatles and one of the biggest selling pop groups of the 1990s—and the bestselling female group in modern music history.

Their album *Spice* sold 23 million copies, making it the bestselling album by a female group—ever. They had nine number-one single hits in England and America and sold in excess of 80 million records. They were also distinctive because they adopted "stage names," such as Posh Spice (Victoria Beckham), Baby Spice, Ginger Spice, Sporty Spice, and Scary Spice (Mel B). Prince Harry and Prince William were big fans of the Spice Girls. At his boarding school, Prince William reportedly took down a poster of Pamela Anderson and replaced it with one of Baby Spice.

Girl Power!

"YOU CAN'T JUST SIT THERE AND WAIT FOR PEOPLE TO GIVE YOU THAT GOLDEN DREAM. YOU'VE GOT TO GET OUT THERE AND MAKE IT HAPPEN FOR YOURSELF."

—DIANA ROSS

Yep, girl power, as projected by great pop stars like the Spice Girls and Korean girl group Wonder Girls, as well as solo superstars like

Katy Perry, Fergie, Pink, Alicia Keys, and, of course, Madonna. It's the special blend of sassiness, irreverence, and confidence that can inspire musicians and nonmusicians alike to unleash their own inner girl power!

Some girls amp up their inner girl power by creating onstage personas, dressing or acting in ways that make them feel even bolder. When the somewhat shy Beyoncé stepped out of the relative safety of being a member of Destiny's Child and went solo, she created Sasha Fierce. She credits Sasha Fierce with the ability to wear those wild outfits, dance, and perform in large arenas.

KIDZ BOP Spotlight: Katy Perry Goes Pop!

"I HAD A VERY STRONG VISION AND SOME RECORD COMPANIES DIDN'T LIKE THAT, BUT I WAITED FOR THE RIGHT ONE AND TOOK A CHANCE. I WAS LUCKY BECAUSE IT DOESN'T ALWAYS PAY OFF."

—KATY PERRY

Katy Perry began her career as a gospel singer, but when she went mainstream pop, she created a sassy persona, visible in her campy clothes and attitude. She wanted an image that let everyone know she was talented and serious, but out there to have fun—and to make herself unforgettable.

Faves...

1. Spice Girls
2. Wonder Girls
3. Bananarama
4. The Bangles
5. The Go-Gos
6. The Donnas

7. The Supremes
8. Luscious Jackson
9. The Runaways

KIDZ BOP Girl Group Song

KIDZ BOP Kid Hanna chooses her faves:

- ★ "Wannabe" by Spice Girls
- ★ "Nobody" by Wonder Girls
- ★ "Cruel Summer" by Bananarama
- ★ "Walk Like an Egyptian" by the Bangles
- ★ "We Got the Beat" by the Go-Gos
- ★ "Fall Behind Me" by the Donnas
- ★ "Stop in the Name of Love" by the Supremes
- ★ "Hollywood" by the Runaways

KIDZ BOP Says: From Asia, With Love

Japanese girl groups have been wildly popular since the late 1990s. One girl group, Speed, sold 20 million copies in Japan alone, and, thanks to the Internet, some, like J-Pop, earned international fame. Korea also has several girl groups that are rocking the airwaves. Girls' Generation, which has nine members between the ages of nineteen and twenty-one, are known for their image and choreography, which has launched fashion trends in Asia and the United States. Some of their songs include, "Tell Me Your Wish," "Gee," "Oh!", "Run Devil Run," and "Hoot."

KIDZ BOP Kids: Choirs and Glee Clubs Rock!

That's right . . . thanks to the success of the TV show *Glee*, as well as the Nick Lachey–hosted holiday series *The Sing-Off*, choir types—singers with incredible voices and the skills to make them sound fantastic even without instrumental accompaniment—are finally getting their props!

Gleeking for Fun and Profit

Do you have glee club or choir pals you'd like to form a band with? Or do you want to start a band because you don't have a glee club? As the Fox TV show and the many hit songs the show's stars have enjoyed on iTunes prove, music fans are digging the *Glee*-ful sounds of vocal harmonizing paired with great pop songs, and that makes this the perfect time for you to unleash your inner Gleek!

KIDZ BOP *Glee* Songs

KIDZ BOP Kid Charisma, who sings in an a cappella group back home, chooses her faves:

- ★ "Don't Stop Believin'"
- ★ "Take a Bow"
- ★ "Somebody to Love"
- ★ "No Air"
- ★ "Jessie's Girl"
- ★ "Empire State of Mind"
- ★ "Total Eclipse of the Heart"

KIDZ BOP Kids: Garage Band

Start with rock, throw in some punk influence, and round up a group of musicians who not only sing and write songs, but also know their way around musical instruments and you've got yourself a rockin' garage band.

KIDZ BOP NOTES: WHY ARE THEY CALLED "GARAGE BANDS"?

It's a retro term, first coined "garage rock" because most of the group members were young and amateurish, and often rehearsed in one of their parents' garage. These bands' music was often much cruder than their inspirations, but it was usually full of the passion and energy that comes from being young and excited about what you're doing. Many couldn't even play an instrument when they formed the band, so most of the bands used simple chord progressions, pounding drums, and catchy lyrics.

Who are some of the bands you should look to for inspiration if rocking out is your thing?

The Rock Gods: Rockin' Inspiration for Aspiring Rock (Band) Stars

Here are Steffan's picks for best rock bands:

1. Green Day
2. Fall Out Boy
3. Metro Station
4. Vampire Weekend
5. The Beatles
6. The Rolling Stones
7. Queen
8. Muse
9. Daughtry
10. David Cook

The World's Most Famous Garage Band

The world's most famous garage band formed around a young man who could barely play a banjo, who gathered a group of friends, none of whom could play an instrument, and formed a group that became the

Quarrymen. It was the late 1950s, and the instigator of the band was one John Lennon. "I just had to show up with my drum kit, that was the audition," said Colin Hanton, one of Lennon's friends who joined up. The breakthrough to fame began when Paul McCartney came on board, and Lennon and McCartney began writing songs together.

Tune Time: Songs You Should Know

★ "Thnks fr th Mmrs" by Fall Out Boy
★ "Radioactive" by Kings of Leon
★ "I Want to Hold Your Hand" by the Beatles
★ "We Are the Champions" by Queen
★ "It's Not Over" by Daughtry
★ "The Time of My Life" by David Cook

Where the Musicians Are

We've established that it's perfectly possible to launch a pop/rock career without being able to play an instrument. But what if you do want to form a rock band, a group whose members will sing, probably write their own music, and definitely play their own instruments? Well, cool!

Who Plays What Well

"MOST BEGINNERS WANT TO LEARN LEAD BECAUSE THEY THINK IT'S COOL . . . CONSEQUENTLY, THEY NEVER REALLY DEVELOP GOOD RHYTHM SKILLS . . . SINCE MOST OF A ROCK GUITARIST'S TIME IS SPENT PLAYING RHYTHM, IT'S IMPORTANT TO LEARN TO DO IT WELL . . . LEARNING LEAD SHOULD COME AFTER YOU CAN PLAY SOLID BACKUP AND HAVE THE SOUND OF THE CHORDS IN YOUR HEAD."

—EDDIE VAN HALEN

But how do you decide who'll play what in the group? The obvious place to start is to determine if any of the group members already know how to play an instrument. If they do, even if it's at a beginner level, run with it! And if you have only one or two band members with musical experience, or even if no one does, don't let that deter you. Discuss which instruments everyone is interested in, and if you're budget-conscious, consider finding used instruments at such places as:

★ Consignment shops
★ Yard sales
★ Swap meets
★ Online classifieds (ask your parents for help here)

You can also check out inexpensive retailers. And don't forget to sign up for lessons!

KIDZ BOP Says: Go-Go Play an Instrument

In the early days, most girl groups sang, but didn't play instruments. The Go-Gos made a splash in the 1980s when they formed an all-girl band that did it all.

Minimum for Rock Bands

★ One to three singers
★ Two to three guitarists (one lead, one rhythm, one bass)
★ A drummer

Optional

★ One pianist, could be an electric keyboardist
★ Violinist
★ Bass
★ Anything else you want

Every band needs instruments, but where to start? First, have a band meeting to discuss who has what and where you need to fill in. The equipment you buy will depend on the type of music you want to play, and how much you can afford. Buying high-quality equipment is desirable, but you can buy something less expensive until you get rolling. Whatever you do, spend a lot of time researching (online or by visiting stores) before you purchase.

In general, to get started you'll need:

Guitars: It all depends on your budget. Good starter guitars ($200–$300) include Fender's foreign-made Stratocasters, Epiphone, PRS, Ibanez, and Washburn. If you've got more to spend, lucky you! Try a Gibson or an American-made Stratocaster, an upper-end Ibanez, or PRS. Affordable acoustic guitars include: Yamaha, Washburn, and Fender.

Drums: It's best to start with kits that include everything—five-piece drum sets, cymbals, sticks, hardware, and even a drum throne (seat). Expensive sets will come with more options, sound better, be sturdier, and last longer than cheap drum sets, but you can start small and grade up later. (Thanks, Mom!)

PA equipment: This basically means speakers (large, small, and foldback speakers). This gets very complicated, so research online or go to music stores and learn as much as you can before you purchase. You can often find used equipment that will work fine to start off.

A sound mixer to plug everything into: Again, this is complicated stuff, so find yourself somebody—like your dad—who's into sound systems and can help set you up.

KIDZ BOP Says: Use a PA System

Think about running everyone through the PA system to create a good overall sound. The notion that PA systems are only for vocalists is not true. Plug everyone into the PA system and make sure that you learn or find someone who knows how to work the mixing unit.

Here's how to make your instruments blend well:

Lead Guitarist: Amp up the volume during lead breaks.

Bass Guitar: Follows the drummer's bass drum.

Rhythm Guitar: Should be lower volume than lead guitar.

Drummer: Needs a foldback amplifier and speakers nearby so they can hear the band in front of them.

Vocalist: It's all about focusing on the vocalist; his or her voice should always be clear and slightly louder, so it is not competing with the instruments.

Keep all volumes on your guitars slightly lower, as it prevents feedback.

Get very comfortable with your equipment before you try a live gig.

KIDZ BOP Says: What Makes a Great Band

★ Talent, talent, talent, and more talent
★ A lead singer with a distinctive voice
★ Versatility: being able to play more than one instrument
★ Being in tune with each other's style
★ Understanding how all the instruments blend
★ Being able to create a unified sound together
★ Being able to create your own arrangements
★ Being able to write your own songs
★ An original, genre-expanding sound

★ A winning stage presence
★ Chemistry, empathy, patience, team spirit
★ Passion for what you're doing
★ The ability to promote yourselves
★ An appreciation for your fans

KIDZ BOP Notes: Must-Know Musicians

If you're forming a band, knowing as much as possible about those who have come before you can give you a real leg up. There are, of course, thousands of really talented musicians, and you can explore by sampling all kinds of music and tuning in to those who play your chosen instrument. Here are a few lists of some of the all-time greats to get you started:

Lead Guitarists

★ John Mayer, singer-songwriter
★ Nick Jonas, of the Jonas Brothers
★ Jack White of the White Stripes
★ John Lee Hooker, no one did the blues like Hooker
★ Curtis Mayfield, known for his unique chords
★ B. B. King, blues guitarist
★ Jimi Hendrix, the man played with his teeth!
★ Eric Clapton, considered one of the best lead guitarists in rock
★ Jimmy Page, Led Zeppelin's superstar
★ Jeff Beck, a rock star guitarist
★ Carlos Santana, created a whole new sound
★ Eddie Van Halen, known for his lightning speed and innovative two-handed fretboard tapping

★ Keith Richards, guitar legend of The Rolling Stones
★ Robert Johnson
★ Chuck Berry
★ The Edge, of Irish rock band U2
★ Bonnie Raitt, one of the best female blues guitarists
★ Joan Jett, a real rocker on guitar

> "I GREW UP IN A WORLD THAT TOLD GIRLS THEY COULDN'T PLAY ROCK 'N' ROLL."
>
> —JOAN JETT

Bass Guitarists

★ Divinity Roxx (plays with Beyoncé and Victor Wooten)
★ Victor Wooten (winner of five Grammies and the first person to win bass Player of the Year more than once)
★ Tony Kanal (No Doubt)
★ James Jamerson (Funk Brothers)
★ Larry Graham (Sly and the Family Stone)
★ Charles Mingus (jazz)
★ Paul McCartney (the Beatles)
★ Jack Bruce (Cream)
★ John Entwistle (the Who)
★ John Paul Jones (Led Zeppelin)
★ Michael "Flea" Balzary (Red Hot Chili Peppers)
★ Mark Hoppus (Blink 182)

Drummers

- ★ Justin Bieber
- ★ Travis Barker (Blink 182)
- ★ Sheila E
- ★ Tommy Lee
- ★ Tico Torres (Bon Jovi)
- ★ Cindy Blackwell (plays with Lenny Kravitz)
- ★ Buddy Guy
- ★ Ginger Baker (Cream)
- ★ Ringo Starr (the Beatles)
- ★ Mick Fleetwood (Fleetwood Mac)
- ★ Phil Collins (Genesis)
- ★ Neil Peart (Rush)
- ★ Danny Carey (Tool)

"I BECAME A DRUMMER BECAUSE IT WAS THE ONLY THING I COULD DO."

—RINGO STARR

Piano/Keyboard Players

- ★ Ray Charles, one of the best piano players—ever!
- ★ Billy Joel, the original "piano man"
- ★ Tori Amos
- ★ Alicia Keys
- ★ Lisa Harriton (The Smashing Pumpkins)
- ★ Norah Jones
- ★ Matt Johnson (Matt & Kim)
- ★ Ben Folds
- ★ Cat Power

★ Herbie Hancock
★ Billy Preston
★ Ray Manzarek (the Doors)
★ Al Kooper (Blood, Sweat and Tears)
★ Keith Emerson (ELP)
★ Peter Gabriel
★ Stevie Wonder
★ Gregg Allman (Allman Brothers Band)
★ Jimmy Greenspoon (Three Dog Night)
★ David Sanscious (Springsteen, Santana, Sting)
★ Brian Eno

Bands

★ The Beatles
★ The Rolling Stones
★ Pink Floyd
★ Red Hot Chili Peppers
★ Nirvana
★ Dave Matthews Band
★ Pearl Jam
★ Radiohead

"WHEN I FIRST FELL IN LOVE WITH THE PIANO, I KNEW IT WAS ME. I WAS DYING TO PLAY."

—ALICIA KEYS

Female Guitarists Who Rock

★ Jennifer Batten (who worked with Michael Jackson on his tours)
★ Kim and Kelley Deal (talented guitar-playing sisters)
★ Lita Ford (former lead guitarist for the Runaways)
★ Marnie Stern (often compared to Eddie Van Halen)
★ Orianthi (who played in Michael Jackson's band)

KIDZ BOP Spotlight on: Girl Guitarist Orianthi

> "BEING A FEMALE GUITAR PLAYER WASN'T EASY. I'VE BEEN PLAYING SINCE I WAS 6 AND PLAYING IN THE SCHOOL BANDS AND GOING FOR AUDITIONS AND LINING UP NEXT TO THE GUYS . . . SOME GUYS THOUGHT IT WAS COOL AND IT WAS PRETTY MUCH THE MALE DRUMMERS. GUITAR PLAYERS DIDN'T TAKE TO IT TOO WELL."
>
> —ORIANTHI

The 24-year-old Australian wunderkind Orianthi has taken the rock world by storm—and proven beyond the shadow of a strum that girl guitarists truly rock! The singer-songwriter's shredding skill is so great that she has been lauded by such legendary guitarists as Carlos Santana, who says about Orianthi: "If I was going to pass the baton to someone, she would be my first choice."

Orianthi has shared the stage with Carlos Santana, as well as Carrie Underwood, Steve Vai, and Michael Jackson. She's also a recording artist in her own right—and of course her first hit single, "According to You," features a fabulous guitar solo. So shred on, Ori!

"When you get up on stage, some of the guys are crossing their arms and saying, 'What are you gonna do?' Now I get up there and just play. I hope to inspire a lot more female guitar players. Just pick it up and keep on going."

—Orianthi

KIDZ BOP Says: Brand Your Band

What does it mean to "brand" your band? It's the same as branding anything, like a clothing line or a videogame. When you hear the name KIDZ BOP, you know what to expect, what kind of music to expect, what the CD label is going to look like, even what kind of talented kids are going to be singing the songs. All those things make up the KIDZ BOP brand.

Think of your favorite restaurant. Odds are, whenever you go into one, you know what to expect of the menu. You know exactly how your favorite dish is going to taste and smell, what the wait staff will be wearing, how the tables will be set, or how the take-out bags will look—logo and all—if you're getting home delivery. It's a unique dining experience unlike any other restaurant—and you can always count on it to be that same way. All those things make up the restaurant's brand, the things you associate with the company when you think of it.

And that's what you want to do with your band . . . brand your band—create a cohesive plan for the band that makes certain things spring to mind when people think of the band.

This plan should reflect you and your band: Do you like to rock out? Are you a stylish showstopper? Is it all about the beat for your dance band?

What are those things that reflect you and your band?

Things That Make Up Your Band's Identitiy

* ★ The name of the band
* ★ The type of music you play
* ★ The type of songs you play—are you a rock band that mostly sings power ballads? Or are you a pop band that mostly plays danceable tunes, for example?
* ★ Your band members' fashion style
* ★ Your band logo
* ★ Your performance style: Do you sing? Do you sing and dance? Do you have elaborately choreographed numbers in your performances?
* ★ Do you play all original music, or are you mostly a cover band, or do you play a mix of both?
* ★ Do you play long, ninety-minute sets, or shorter sets?
* ★ Who's your audience? Do you play school functions? Do you perform at church events? Or kiddie birthday parties? Do you have aspirations of playing outside the local area? Are you looking to travel across your state, across the country to perform?
* ★ The way you promote the band—your press kit, posters, fliers, T-shirts, stickers, and other swag
* ★ Your band bio
* ★ Your band photo
* ★ And, of course, your band website, KIDZBOP.com, and all of the other social networking sites . . .

What branding really boils down to is when someone hires your band for a gig, what are they getting? In order to get hired, you have to make very clear what your band is bringing to the table, and that starts with your band name, which should fit in with the overall image you're trying to project.

Here are some fun ideas to help you create a killer band name!

★ Visit Bandnamemaker.com, where you enter a random word and the site generates several band name suggestions.

★ Combine the name of your first pet with the name of your favorite fruit. Ours would be Yoyo Strawberry!

★ Use a phrase from your all-time favorite book.

★ Consider what kind of music your band will play. For instance, if you're a pop group that sings mostly sweet love songs, The Smelly Socks is probably not the best way for you to go. On the flip side, if you're a heavy metal rock band, Little Bunny Foo Foo is probably not a great band name for you. Actually, we kinda like that one. . . .

★ Use the name to honor someone really important in your life.

★ Use a word or phrase from a foreign language.

★ Combine the name of your favorite color with the name of your favorite amusement park or carnival ride. Ours: Fuchsia Ferris Wheel.

★ Combine the first letter of each band member's first, middle, or last name. That's how ABBA—with band members Agnetha, Björn, Benny, and Anni-Frid—came up with their band name.

Clothes Count (Even for the Drummer!)

> "BEING IN A BAND YOU CAN WEAR WHATEVER YOU WANT—IT'S LIKE AN EXCUSE FOR HALLOWEEN EVERY DAY."
>
> —GWEN STEFANI

By which we mean, yes, the drummer is sitting behind his kit for the whole performance, but you wouldn't want him to sit there in his pajamas and slippers, right? So, if clothing matters for the guy or girl hidden behind a big set of drums, fashion for the band members who are more front and center definitely matter.

First and foremost is that you're comfortable in what you wear, both from a physical comfort point of view and a fashion point of view. If you're a girl who never wears skirts or shoes with a higher heel, the stage probably isn't the place to start, especially when you're going to be moving and grooving a lot. If you're a preppier guy, studded belts, leather pants, and black fingernail polish probably isn't going to settle so well with you.

But do be open to trying new things. That's the key. If you're a jeans and T-shirt kinda guy, choose colorful tees with interesting quotes or photos or graphics on them. Pair them with a vest. Make your jeans any color but blue. Pull it all together with a great hat or some funky kicks.

For girls, pair a knee-length dress with tights or denim leggings. Wear several different colors. Hair accessories and jewelry . . . the funkier the better. Pick something and make it your signature; be the girl who always wears cool tights, in different colors and patterns. Wear ties with your T-shirts or tops. Scour chain stores, vintage clothing shops, yard sales, and other discount retailers for cocktail rings or great brooches you can pair with pretty shirts and jeans, for a shabby chic look.

To sum it all up, when you think about your band fashions:

★ Be comfy.
★ Be creative.
★ Wear color.
★ Make it interesting.
★ Be unique.
★ Try to develop a signature look.
★ Have fun with fashion.
★ Express yourself!

How Inspiring! Superstar Examples of Great Band Branding

Check out this roundup of bands with great names, and consider how well the name suits the band you know them to be . . . their band logos, their CD covers, their videos, tours, their clothing, even the band merch like T-shirts and posters. It all makes sense, right? Think about all those things when you choose your band name!

1. U2
2. KISS
3. Rolling Stones
4. Sonic Youth
5. Nirvana
6. Guns 'n Roses
7. They Might Be Giants
8. Kings of Leon
9. Electric Light Orchestra
10. Metallica
11. Queen
12. Spice Girls
13. Muse
14. 'N Sync
15. Green Day
16. Fall Out Boy
17. 3 Doors Down
18. Bananarama
19. Sunny Day Real Estate
20. Foo Fighters
21. The Wallflowers
22. Oingo Boingo
23. Duran Duran
24. Gnarls Barkley
25. The Yeah Yeah Yeahs
26. Smashing Pumpkins

27. Talking Heads
28. Culture Club
29. Plain White T's
30. No Doubt
31. Owl City
32. Tokio Hotel

Who's on First

Like every business, or group activity, a band needs one thing first and foremost: a leader!

The Leader of the Band

> "EACH ONE OF YOU HAS SOMETHING NO ONE ELSE HAS, OR HAS EVER HAD: YOUR FINGERPRINTS, YOUR BRAIN, YOUR HEART. BE AN INDIVIDUAL. BE UNIQUE. STAND OUT. MAKE NOISE. MAKE SOMEONE NOTICE. THAT'S THE POWER OF INDIVIDUALS."
>
> —JON BON JOVI

Every band needs a band leader. Seriously: There has to be one leader, one person who is the glue that keeps the whole operation running.

Have you ever hung out with a group of friends, trying to decide what to do on a Saturday afternoon? One person suggests going to the movies, another wants to go to the mall food court, another wants to go to a friend's house and play Xbox, and another says he doesn't care what you do. The result: You all spend the next hour waiting for some-one to make a strong enough case so that everyone will eventually agree to do something—anything! Instead, if someone had stepped up and taken the lead, and said, "Hey, why don't we go see a movie at the mall, and then go to the food court afterward?" you would have been on your way to a fun afternoon, instead of sitting around trying to decide what to do.

And that's why your band needs a leader. There will be a million and one decisions to make as a band—which songs you'll sing, what you'll wear onstage, whose name will be listed first in the band bio, which publicity photo you'll include in your band press kit, whose turn it is to stay after practice and tidy up your rehearsal space, who's going to bring snacks for the next rehearsal, and on and on and on.

Enter: You! You can do it! Sure, being a good leader is a skill, but it's one you can learn—and one that will carry over into the rest of your life, for the rest of your life. A few tips on how to make sure you're at the top of your game as a leader. . . .

Eleven Ways to Be a Good Leader

1. Be a good listener. In fact, being a leader often means more listening than talking. If people believe their voice is being heard, it can smooth over most any disagreement.

2. Lead by example. Say you've got a band member who's always late for practice. As the leader of the band it's your job to talk to her about it, so you'd better be on time yourself!

3. Be on top of your game. If you haven't learned all the lyrics to the new song the band's going to be singing at your next gig, why should anyone else?

4. Be understanding. Life happens, sometimes not the way we want it to, and everyone, including you, will have to make accommodations for other band members sometimes (just as they will have to occasionally make them for you).

5. Be friendly, but fair, with everyone. You may be, in fact, probably will be, closer to some bandmates than to others. But when you're making decisions for the group, you need to put your personal friendships aside and do what's in the best interest of the group.

6. Arrange social gatherings occasionally, where you're not doing band work but just having fun and getting to know each other better. The more you hang out together, the better you'll know each other, and the more sensitive you'll each be to everyone else's needs and desires for the band.

7. Constructive criticism only! Lead with a compliment before dropping a bit of negative feedback. Example: "Joelly, thank you so much for designing those incredible posters for our concert at the school assembly next week. We totally appreciate it! Could you try to make sure you're on time for rehearsal tomorrow, though, because we all have midterm exams and need to get home to study?"

8. Be organized.

9. Be committed. If you're not, you have no chance of keeping everyone else committed to the band.

10. When you do need to talk to one of your band members about something he or she might not want to hear, do it privately. So have that conversation about being late all the time behind closed doors—it's the respectful thing to do!

11. Chill out. When you do get angry or frustrated with your bandmates— and you will, at some point, get angry or frustrated with your bandmates, and vice versa—walk away for a few minutes, count to 100, recite the alphabet to yourself, think about rainbows and puppies . . . in other words, take a time-out and calm yourself down before you react in any way. This way you won't overreact—or say something you might regret later. As leader of the band you set the tone—and you want it to be a tone of goodwill, cooperation, and respect. Not to mention fun!

> "I WRITE THE MUSIC, PRODUCE IT, AND THE BAND PLAYS WITHIN THE PARAMETERS THAT I SET."
>
> —STING

Jammin' on the Same Page: How to Keep Your Group Jammin' Together!

★ Have regular band meetings. Once a week? Once a month? Whatever the frequency, make sure it's a regular thing. It keeps everyone's commitment to your project fresh.

★ At those meetings, make the first order of business asking everyone if there are issues to discuss. Making sure everyone's voice is heard sets a good tone for the rest of the meeting.

★ A band, or any group working together on the same project, will be made up of different personalities. Everyone has to respect that from the beginning, and learn to communicate with each other while being sensitive to the differences.

★ Hold brainstorming sessions for new song ideas, costumes, and ways to promote the band and get new jobs.

★ Encourage each other's outside interests. You want the band members to be close and committed to the group, but everyone has other friends and interests outside the band, obviously, and by acknowledging and encouraging that, it will create an environment where everyone respects and cares about each other.

★ Check out other bands together! Talk about music, the music you all love, and the music that individual members may like. It will help inspire everyone and make sure you all continue to be excited about this thing of yours!

★ Occasionally re-evaluate your band's goals. Are you all still on the same page regarding the kind of music you're playing, your rehearsal schedule, how frequently you're booking jobs, your publicity efforts?

★ If there's one member of the band who just isn't jelling with the other members, personally or musically, consider replacing him or her. Be kind and polite about it if you do ultimately decide the person has to go, but honestly evaluate what's best for the group and make the decision together.

★ Practice, practice, practice. Sounds obvious, but sometimes you can get so bogged down with the business of being a band, and dealing with the many personalities within the group, that you lose focus on what got you all together in the first place: the music! There's no point in pursuing this whole music thang if you don't love music, so a great band rehearsal can be just the thing to keep everyone on or get everyone back to the same page, with an excited attitude and commitment to the band.

KIDZ BOP KIDS ON: OUR STORY

STEFFAN: "We have meetings at least once a week, sometimes more often if we have a particularly busy schedule. It's important, because things can get way out of control if we don't make sure we sit down together and talk at least once a week."

HANNA: "Sometimes we'll just do silly things, and it can help break us out of a stressful situation. Like, Eva will pass around a Bop It! or Elijah will do these crazy impersonations. Little things like that just make us laugh at just the right time."

EVA: "We all have totally different personalities, but that's what makes us so great! Why would we want a group with five copies of the same person? You just have to be really respectful about the way you talk to each other, especially if you're having a disagreement."

ELIJAH: "Being in a pop group is a lot of hard work, and it makes it more fun to be in the band with my friends. Even when we argue about something, or we're all so tired and have a ton of homework to do and just want to be at home, I can't imagine this experience without any of them."

CHARISMA: "We may have little moments where we get frustrated with each other, like if we're really stressed out, but this is the most fun job in the world, and we all really care about each other and want the best for each other, so we always work it out pretty quickly. Plus, we can all make each other laugh!"

Rock Your Rehearsals

Because your music isn't the only thing in your life, you've got to make the time you do spend on it count. And one of the most obvious ways to do that is to make your band rehearsals über-productive.

That can be easier said than done, of course; it's one thing to get yourself to rehearsal on time and ready to rock, but being in a band means getting everyone ready to go at the same time. Challenge!

But, as with most aspects of your pop stardom, and especially with being part of a band, the key is organization. Don't just show up for rehearsal; come prepared!

Five Steps for a Productive Band Rehearsal

1. Check your moods at the door. You had a bad day. Your drummer got a D on his algebra exam. Your keyboardist had a fight with his older brother right before practice. It happens, but if everyone brings their personal problems into rehearsal time, it will affect your bandmates negatively, and it's just not fair to indulge your mood and waste their time.

2. Come prepared with your instrument or sheet music or lyrics sheet or whatever your musical accoutrements happen to be. Sounds obvious, but every minute it takes you to do something that should have been ready to go the minute you stepped into rehearsal is a minute of your bandmates' time that you are stealing from them. Not cool.

3. Be open to new ideas. Doesn't mean you have to implement all, or any, of them ultimately, but the only way the band will grow creatively is to be open to new things, especially during rehearsals, which is the time to try new things.

4. Come with an agenda. Every member of the band should know exactly what is to be accomplished during each rehearsal. Is today's rehearsal about preparing for a specific upcoming show? Is the rehearsal you have planned for the weekend to make sure everyone has learned the choreography you've planned for a new song? Need to work out some sketchy lyrics before you can debut that new love song you wrote last week? Setting specific goals for each rehearsal will ensure those things get done.

5. Focus. Wanna talk about that great movie you just saw or the hot guy who sits behind you in American history class or what you're going to buy your best friend for her birthday? Cool . . . but do it after rehearsal. Even if you have a band business issue to discuss, do it after rehearsal. Band meetings are for discussing band business; rehearsals are for actually rehearsing your music and performance.

Mix It Up: Covers and Original Songs

"I'M NOT REALLY A SONGWRITER . . . I'M AN INTERPRETER. SO IN A SENSE I AM AN ACTRESS FIRST AND FOREMOST. I ACT OUT THE SONGS, AND I LEAD WITH MY HEART."

—DIANA ROSS

You already know that KIDZ BOP is all about the cover tunes . . . it's what we do! And there are a lot of bands who also do that very thing, even brand their band around the idea of covering songs of one specific performer. You've heard of tribute bands, right? There are Elvis Presley tribute performers, Beatles tribute bands, Rolling Stones tribute bands . . . name pretty much any superstar musical act of the last fifty years, and it's a good bet that there's a band somewhere that's forging its own musical career by paying tribute to that superstar band's music.

Meanwhile, the majority of pop superstars find success by singing original tunes, whether it's songs they write themselves or songs they pay other people to write.

Which your group does depends on a few things, the first one being whether or not there's anyone in the group who can write music. We covered writing songs on your own in Part Two, but you can also try writing songs as a group.

KIDZ BOP Jammin' Band Writing Session

Start with a group writing session. Ask each band member to come with some ideas—poetry they've written, a great line that just sticks in their head, or maybe an issue that they feel really strongly about that they could put into a song. Here are some hints:

1. Love. A good romance or love gone wrong—both have provided songwriters with inspiration since the beginning of songwriting history.
2. Your journal or diary.
3. An issue that's important to you, like kindness to animals or the environment.
4. Silly words or phrases, or just a word that you like. We love the word "doppelganger" . . . it's a fun word to say, right? Flip through a dictionary or thesaurus and write down some words that catch your eye.
5. Write a parody of a popular song. Weird Al Yankovic has made a very successful career out of it—he's hilarious!
6. Write about someone really important to you . . . your aunt, your grandpa, your best friend, your dog!
7. Your favorite book, movie, TV show, videogame, comic book, etc.
8. How much you love/hate algebra/gym class or whatever your favorite or least favorite class is.
9. The worst day of your life.
10. The best day of your life.

When you get together, throw around your ideas, and see which ones stick. Use your instruments, and encourage improvisation. Keep it low-key, so nobody gets uptight. You want the music to flow! And remember to provide lots of snacks and drinks—you can't create on an empty stomach!

Once Again, with Energy!

"SOMETIMES THIS IS THE MOST FUN EVER. OTHER TIMES IT'S REALLY HARD AND THERE'S SO MUCH PRESSURE."

—JUSTIN BIEBER

Practice, practice, practice . . . if you think the idea of playing the same songs over and over again doesn't sound like fun, being a pop star may not be for you, after all. Once you know a song really well, you're going to have to perform it again and again. And once it becomes a hit, you're going to have to perform it again and again . . . for the rest of your career! But before any of that can happen, you're going to have to play the same songs again and again to learn how to play them (again and again!).

Rehearsals can seem like a chore, and especially when some members of the band may learn things at a different (read: slower) pace than the other members, it can be frustrating. But you know what's far, far worse: showing up for a gig, unprepared to perform, or performing so badly that you don't get a second shot.

So . . . practice, practice, practice!

How Tight Is Your Band?

Here's the thing: the members of your band? They don't have to be your best friends. They certainly don't have to be your only friends. But your whole musical career experience will be a lot more entertaining if you and your bandmates get along. And if they happen to be your best friends, well, that's certainly not a bad thing, right?

Get Along to Sing Along

Drama . . . fun when it's happening on the movie screen or on TV, not so fun when you find yourself in the middle of it. And that can happen oh so easily when you're part of a group of performers, each with his or her own personality, goals, and agenda for how your band should run. So, how do you maneuver your way through all those competing factors to make sure your musical dreams don't end in one giant rehearsal fight before you even play your first gig? It's actually a pretty simple idea: respect.

When you're in a discussion with someone, and the discussion turns heated, what is the number-one most frustrating thing the other person can do? Not listen to you, right? Everyone gets excited, everyone's passionate about their own ideas, and sometimes that turns a discussion into a fight, where voices are raised, feelings are hurt and—worst possible scenario—people say things they might not mean.

The solution? Fight nice. You know how your parents and teachers have always told you to play nice? Well, you should fight the same way!

Mind Your Manners: How to Fight the Good Fight (and Keep the Band Together)

1. No name calling. Ever.
2. Think before you speak. There's a little filter between what pops into your head and what actually leaves your mouth . . . make sure that filter is working at all times, especially when you're angry or frustrated.
3. Walk before you speak. If you don't think you can have a rational discussion without yelling and name calling, take a walk. It is not going out on a limb at all to say that thousands, at least thousands, of bands

could have been saved if their members had just taken a short time-out instead of launching into an all-out, band-ending war with each other.

4. Do unto others. Always works . . . do not treat anyone in a way that you would not like them to treat you.

5. Consider others' ideas. No matter how wacky it may initially seem, genuinely think about the other person's viewpoint or idea. It's a lot easier to come to a compromise when everyone feels like they have at least been heard and given consideration.

6. Don't gang up on each other. It's the beginning of the end of the group if you start splitting into groups within the group and then butting heads.

7. If you can't resolve an issue, consider bringing in a third person—NOT someone else in the band!—to hear both sides and see if they can shed some new, impartial light on it.

8. Be open, but be firm. If you really believe in something, and you're sure you're being fair and respectful in presenting it, don't be bullied into dropping it. One, if it's truly a great idea, you may just need to convince your bandmates that it's a great idea. Two, if you feel bullied into changing your mind, you'll grow resentful, and that just leads to even bigger clashes down the road.

9. Don't be a bully!

10. Keep in mind that not every issue will be resolved, and certainly not every issue will be resolved with one discussion. It may take a while to work out certain issues. It is most likely going to be resolved by compromise on everyone's part.

Nine Ways to Make Sure Your Band Keeps on Rockin'

1. Be polite.

2. Don't hold back, though. Say what's on your mind, but always in a respectful way.

3. Remember that everyone, not just you, has a life outside the band.

4. Be on time, for everything. Nothing will tick off your bandmates more than actions by you that indicate you think your time is more valuable than theirs is.

5. Don't let egos spin out of control. If you think one of your bandmates is demanding too much of the spotlight, call a meeting and get the issue out in the open right away. Letting jealousy and resentment over such matters fester is what has broken up all too many great bands.

6. Teasing is fun, but there are limits. Everybody has their issues, things that are hot-button, sensitive matters to them. That means, no matter how playful your intentions might be, don't press those buttons. We all have them, so we all know how not fun it is to be teased when you just don't feel like being teased.

7. Hang out together outside band meetings and rehearsals.

8. But be careful about starting romances with your bandmates. It's a potential mine field, and if you break up . . . well, let's just say bad romances have taken out their fair share of good bands, too.

9. Sounds obvious, but be supportive of one another. Don't be jealous of attention your bandmates get; their success is your success when you're in a band.

How Inspiring! Five Bands That Got It Right

1. Rolling Stones—they may fight, they may not even speak to each other sometimes, but they're still together after all these years (forty-nine years to be exact!).

2. U2—they became a band in Ireland in 1976 and have been together ever since. Best of all: They're still making great tunes, doing incredible charity work, and involving themselves in cool projects like the *Spider-Man* musical on Broadway.

3. ZZ Top—forty-two years together and still rockin' and rollin'.

4. Bon Jovi—Jon Bon Jovi and the band have been together for twenty-eight years, and they're still making some of the best music of their careers and selling out tour dates all over the world.
5. Green Day—the punk rockers have been together for twenty-four years and have sold more than 24 million albums in the United States alone, and in 2010, the Broadway musical adaptation of their bestselling album *American Idiot* won four Tony Awards.

. . . and Five That Broke Up

1. The Beatles—fighting and John Lennon's relationship with Yoko Ono are the supposed reasons for the legendary band's breakup.
2. Blondie—lead singer Debbie Harry got all the attention (and reportedly held all the power) in the band, and the other members refused to stick around and let the situation continue.
3. The Mamas and the Papas—love affairs gone wrong and in-fighting led to the bust up of this '60s pop group.
4. The Clash—fighting and the departure of original band members ultimately led to the group's demise.
5. 'N Sync—lead singer Justin Timberlake's desire for a solo music career and an acting career led to the breakup of this '90s pop superstar boy band.

KIDZ BOP KIDS ON: HOW TIGHT IS YOUR BAND?

STEFFAN: "These guys are my best friends."

HANNA: "We're a band, but we're also like a little KIDZ BOP family, so even though we may get frustrated with each other, we always work it out."

EVA: "I think we all keep in mind how lucky we are to be able to be in this band together, so we're not going to let small things build up and take the fun out of that."

ELIJAH: "We spend time together not even talking about anything related to the band, and that's important. Even if we weren't in the band together, I'd still want to hang out with all of these guys."

CHARISMA: "We can all be pretty loud and we all have our own ideas, but we all really want the group to do well, so we always find a way to compromise and make everyone happy."

PART FOUR

CHAPTER 10

The KIDZ BOP Red Carpet Rules!

> "I ALWAYS THOUGHT I SHOULD BE TREATED LIKE A STAR."
>
> —MADONNA

You know you're a star—and soon the world will know it, too. Life will change forever then—there's no putting the fame and fortune genie back into the bottle. But you can handle success—and enjoy it, too!—when you're prepared for life in the spotlight.

WELCOME TO THE KIDZ BOP RED CARPET RULES!

STEFFAN: "Being a KIDZ BOP Kid is a dream come true—but I wasn't sure how I'd feel about being recognized all the time. It's cool for people to remember you because they liked your singing or your guitar playing. But it's embarrassing when the girls keep asking me about my hair. I mean, it's just hair."

HANNA: "Before I became a KIDZ BOP Kid, only people at home in Colorado would recognize me sometimes, from the local TV commercials I've done for a sporting goods store. But now kids recognize me all the time—usually at the mall. Mom says that it takes a lot longer to shop now, but it's so fun!"

EVA: "The great part about living in New York City is that even when everyone knows who you are, they leave you alone. Superstars and supermodels walk down the streets of Manhattan every day, and nobody ever bothers them. So no matter how famous I get, I'll still have the best of both worlds!"

CHARISMA: "I was a little freaked out about what it would be like to get noticed all the time, but so far all the fans have been very sweet. It helps that when we go out as the KIDZ BOP Kids, we're all together, and we look out after each other. It's fun!"

ELIJAH: "The first time I got recognized, I was in line at the movies with a couple of friends from my school. This cute girl with long red hair and blue eyes came right up to me, stared at me for a minute and then said, 'OMG! You're one of the KIDZ BOP Kids!' Then she started screaming and all her friends ran over, and they started screaming, too! They asked for my autograph, and I signed their ticket stubs because of course I didn't have any photographs to sign. It was awesome! The guys still give me a hard time about it."

Your Public Is Calling!

It can happen overnight. One day only your mom thinks you're a star—and the next day reporters are calling to interview "the world's newest pop star."

This is when the fun *really* starts. Time to get ready to face your public!

When you're talking to any member of the press—newspaper reporter, magazine editor, TV journalist, online columnist—you want to make the most positive impression you can. Here are some KIDZ BOP interview tips that will help you wow the media every time—not to mention help you meet new people and make new friends, wherever you go!

Give Good "Face"!

The camera is on you now—and it's time for your close-up! Most of the time, the focus will be on your face—so here are some DOs and DON'Ts on how to give good "face"!

The Eyes Have It

★ **DO** maintain eye contact with the reporter. You want to look the reporter directly in the eye, and maintain eye contact throughout the interview. This helps you establish a connection with the reporter and shows the reporter that you are paying attention and are interested in the conversation you are sharing.

★ **DON'T** stare directly into the camera. This makes it look like you're not really part of the conversation—and you'll come across as bored (at best) or rude (at worst).

★ **DON'T** sneak peeks at the cameraman, or the lights, or anything else. Keep your eyes on the reporter—or you'll look like you're staring off into space.

You're All Ears

★ **DO** listen. Reporters are looking for a good story—and good quotes—from you during the interview. If you're not listening to the questions, then you won't be able to give good answers. You want to get the reputation of being "a good interview"—and giving a good interview means that you pay close attention to what the interviewer is saying and listen carefully to what the interviewer is asking.

★ **DON'T** start forming the answer in your head while the reporter is still asking the question. You run the risk of missing the point of the question—and answering another point altogether.

★   **DON'T** get distracted by the lights, the cameras, or the other people on set or in the newsroom. Media workplaces tend to be very busy, cramped spaces full of people and equipment—but don't let that throw you. Stay focused on the interviewer—and the interview.

Do Open Mouth, Don't Insert Foot

★   **DO** think before you speak. You may have to fight the impulse to jump right in without thinking, especially if you're nervous. But fight that impulse and think first, because in this technological age, what you say—for better or worse—can live on forever to haunt you and no matter what you may hear to the contrary, nothing you say is really "off the record" anymore, so be careful what you say! ("Off the record" is a term journalists use that means they won't quote you on it . . . but don't count on it!)

★   **DO** speak clearly.

★   **DO** keep your head up and eyes on the interviewer. This will help keep you from mumbling into your collar.

★   **DO** smile, when appropriate. Like your mom always says, you look beautiful when you smile!

★   **DON'T** chew gum. It looks and sounds terrible on camera, not to mention it's rude.

HANNA: "The first time I talked to a TV reporter, it was at a local talent show where I came in first place. I had just grabbed some gum because my mouth was dry after performing. And then this reporter came up to talk to me, and bam! I was on camera. I didn't have time to get rid of the gum—and I couldn't spit it out on camera. So I was stuck—and it was awkward. I got through it, but I never chewed gum again. My mom was really happy about that."

The Rest of You

While the focus is mostly on your face during an interview, the rest of you is important, too. What you're thinking, feeling, and believing during the interview affect how you look and behave—and ultimately how you come across to the press—and to the public.

So here are some DOs and DON'Ts media tips for your mind, body, and spirit.

It's All in Your Mind

★ **DO** be positive! When it comes to your public image, you want to communicate a positive mental attitude (PMA) at all times in every way! Why? Because PMA is contagious—if you've got PMA, odds are so will the interviewer—and that means good press for you!

★ **DO** have fun! After all, you're in the spotlight, as every KIDZ BOP pop star was born to be! You could be home taking out the garbage or doing math homework, but instead you're talking to the press and to your fans. What's not to like?

★ **DON'T** worry. You'll be great—because you've got PMA!

Body Language 101

★ **DO** relax! The more you can chill, the better!

★ **DON'T** tense up your muscles! Consciously relax head to toe, and breathe!

★ **DO** act naturally. You DON'T want to slump, but you DON'T want to sit up at attention either.

★ **DON'T** fidget. Sit still; no playing with your hair or swaying side to side or tapping your foot. Not only will you come across as nervous, you'll also distract your interviewer and your audience from what you are saying. Not to mention that most nervous tics make noise—and that noise is amplified on-set.

Let Your Spirit Shine Through

★ **DO** be yourself! Sure, that's what your mom always tells you, but she's right! This is your opportunity to share your music and let the world know who you really are. Let your warm, smart, confident personality shine!

★ **DO** be nice and gracious. Manners count! And we don't just mean the obvious things, like remembering to thank your interviewer for the interview. We also mean staying upbeat and positive—not just about yourself, but also other people.

★ **DON'T** diss anybody, on camera or off.

CHARISMA: "I'm never shy when I'm onstage performing, but offstage in real life, I can be shy—especially around new people. The first time a reporter called my mom and asked for an interview, I was really nervous about it. I was worried that I would freeze up—and not be able to say anything at all! So before we went to the TV studio, Mom and I did some breathing exercises. It calmed me down—and I did just fine!"

Lights, Camera, *Talk!*

The trick to a great interview is to KISS: Keep It Simple, Superstar!

Before the interview, prepare a few message points that you want to get across. These are things that you want your audience to know, such as:

★ Your new KIDZ BOP webshow is up on KIDZBOP.com.

★ You shot a music video with your band that's up on KIDZBOP .com.

⭐ You're appearing in a local talent show on Friday.
⭐ You just landed the lead in your school musical.
⭐ You'll be modeling on the runway for a local fashion fundraising event next week.

THE KIDZ BOP KIDS ON: INTERVIEW TIPS

STEFFAN: "After I found out that I was going to be KIDZ BOP Kid, my hometown news station called me in for an interview. I wanted to talk about how excited I was to be a KIDZ BOP Kid, but the interviewer kept asking me questions about being a kid in show business. Did I go to school, was I homeschooled, stuff like that. I mean, it was summer—nobody was even in school! But I stayed on point and kept talking about how I got to be a KIDZ BOP Kid, and how any kid who loved to sing and dance and play the guitar could do the same thing I did. And it turned out just fine in the end."

Not all interviews are alike. TV works differently than radio; newspapers and magazines operate by their own rules in turn. Now let's take a look at each kind of interview, so you know how to rock each one!

TV and Radio Interviews

On TV and radio, it's all about time. The producers run everything by the clock—including you! Here's how your time on the set will break down.

The Preinterview

Before the interview, you'll sit down with the show's host or producer to review what you'll be talking about on the air. This is a sort of mini-rehearsal, which typically only lasts a few minutes. But in those few minutes, you'll learn what is expected of you during the interview, and what direction the interviewer plans to take.

Most important, you'll have the opportunity to tell the interviewer what you'd like to talk about during the interview—that is, your message points.

The preinterview is really important—you don't want to miss it! That's why you should always be available at least fifteen minutes early.

The Long—and Short—of Your Interview

TV and radio shows are very tightly scheduled—and every minute counts! If it's a live interview—conducted in real time—then you'll know beforehand approximately how long your interview will last. . . .

Unless everything changes, which can happen in the media business! Breaking news, overbooking, missing guests—these are just a few of the things that can affect your time on the air. So don't be surprised if you end up on the air for a longer or shorter period of time than you expected.

It's All in the Timing

Given the time crunch you're under when you're on the air, you need to make the most of every minute. Here are some time-smart hints:

★ Keep your answers short, concise, and to the point.
★ If it's a live interview, this means limiting your answers to only three or four sentences each.
★ If it's a taped interview that will be edited into sound bites, limit your answers to only twenty seconds each.

WHAT'S A SOUND BITE?

Sound bites are short, memorable comments prized by the media for their brevity and impact.

Before your interview, rehearse delivering your message points in sound bites. Work on making them quick and quotable. Edit yourself ahead of time—so you don't have to leave it to the reporters or producers or editors.

Ready—or Not—You're On!

Be sure that you ask the interviewer to tell you when the interview begins. Otherwise, you run the risk of saying something off the cuff that is not meant for broadcast—but everybody out there will hear. This happens more often than you'd think—so ask! Better safe than sorry!

What to Wear for TV and/or Personal Appearances

And now for the part that you've really been waiting for, that burning question you've been wanting to ask all along: What do I wear?

Of course, you want to wear something fabulous—something that's appropriate and flatters you and looks good on camera. But most important, you want to wear something that you're comfortable in—something that fits you well and feels good on.

This bears repeating: Be comfortable in your outfit! It doesn't matter how cool your outfit is, if you're uncomfortable in it. So don't wear clothes that are too tight, too itchy, too short, *too* anything!

The camera doesn't lie—if you're uncomfortable in any way, it will show. And you don't want to learn that the hard way!

EVA: "My mother's a fashion designer, so she always helps me choose what to wear on camera. She works with lots of models, so she knows how clothes look in photographs and on TV. Mom always tells me to wear something colorful and cheerful, so I look cute and chic at the same time. And she makes me wear the outfit all day the week before to break it in, so I'll know that I feel comfortable in it."

Camera Rules to Live By

Speaking of the camera, here are the rules you need to observe to make sure that the camera captures the best—and not the worst—of you!

1. Assume that the camera and the microphone are on at all times. Get this one wrong, and you could have some serious egg on your face—for all of the world to see!
2. Be alert. Think about what you say and do during the entire process—not just when you think the cameras are rolling.
3. Focus your attention on the person conducting the interview.
4. Don't worry about the shots. It's the cameraperson's job to follow you, and get the shots he or she needs.
5. Stay in your seat, even after you think the interview is over. The interview isn't actually over until the interviewer or the producer tells you it is—and that you're off the air and it's okay for you to get up and go.

Print Interviews

When you do an interview with a newspaper, magazine, online reporter, or blogger, keep in mind that these are professional interviewers who make a living getting people to say things that they don't necessarily want to say in print. Here are some ways to help make sure they get your story right.

★ Think before you speak.
★ Immediately correct any inaccurate statements the reporter makes about you or anything else.
★ Remember: *Nothing* is off the record. Even if you've said it is and the reporter agrees to it. Confidential information is only confidential if you *don't* talk about it.

★ Have fun stories ready to support the message points you want to talk about—if and when appropriate.

★ Restate and rephrase your message points every chance you get during the interview. This ups the odds that the reporter will get them right when they do the story.

★ Speak conversationally—especially when delivering your message points.

Telephone Interviews

Radio and print journalists often do interviews over the telephone. The great thing about these interviews is that you can talk to people all over the world about your performing—without even leaving your living room. But audio alone does present some challenges, so keep the following in mind:

1. Prepare your message points in advance. With no visual to fill in the dead air, you really need to have these down for the interview.
2. If it's a radio interview, use a land line instead of a cell phone. Most radio stations will insist on it, since cell phones can cut out at any time.
3. Feel free to move around. Stand, smile, gesture with your hands. This will animate your voice, so you'll sound livelier, funnier, more interesting to your audience—even though they can't see you!
4. Speak clearly and concisely. You want people to hear and understand everything you say.

HANNA: "I love doing telephone interviews, because I love talking on the phone. I spend a lot of time on the phone with my girlfriends, so I'm really good at it. Plus, you can do a telephone interview any time. You don't have to spend hours getting ready, deciding what to wear, fixing your hair, whatever. Nobody can see you, so you can do interviews in pajamas and a ponytail if you want!"

KIDZ BOP Says: Get the Word Out about *You*!

You know what to do in an interview, but how do you get one? For that, you need to get the word out about you and your talent! There are lots of things you can do to show the world that you're ready for the red carpet!

Let's take a look at the best ways to get the word out about *you*!

Shoot Your Own KIDZ BOP Music Video!

Kids are becoming stars online—like Greyson Chance, Justin Bieber, Charice, Cody Simpson, and our very own Hunter Pecunia, who won the first annual KIDZ Star USA Talent Search.

Shooting a music video is not only a good way to showcase your talent, it's fun! You'll have a great time shooting your video—and, after you post it on KIDZBOP.com, meeting your fellow performers and making all your new fans.

Check out the music videos on the website, and start planning your own! At KIDZ BOP.com, kids post their music videos—and so can you!

STEFFAN: "I made my first music video just for fun. My mom got me a Flip camera for my birthday, and so I just started fooling around with it. I loved the Bruno Mars song 'Just the Way You Are,' so I learned to play it on the guitar and then I had my dad shoot me singing it. I just sat on my bed with my guitar, so it wasn't very complicated, but I cleaned up my room first and hung a lot of cool posters on the wall behind me, so it looked pretty good. And when I posted it on KIDZ BOP, I made a lot of friends—and fans!"

HANNA: "My first music video was me and my BFFs at a sleepover at my house. We didn't plan anything, we were just singing karaoke, and when we got to 'Girls Just Wanna Have Fun,' we went a little crazy, singing and dancing all around the living room. My mom got out the video camera, and we did it all over again. It was awesome—and the music video was pretty cool, too!"

CHARISMA: "My dad videotapes everything our family does—whether we like it or not! But when I told him I wanted to make a music video, he totally helped me. I sang the Taylor Swift song, 'Teardrops on My Guitar.' Dad shot me singing it at home, in the park, even on my horse! Then he edited it all together. He did a great job—and I was thrilled when I got to post it on KIDZ BOP."

EVA: "My mom had all these fashion models over for lunch, and we were just hanging out. I took out my cell phone and started taking pictures. We were all voguing for the camera. Later I got this idea to string them all together in a music video. My brother, who's a total geek, helped me put it together and put in me singing 'Paparazzi' a cappella as the background. It turned out great—and the girls were really sweet about it, letting me use their pix for free!"

ELIJAH: "I love Halloween. So I talked my drama club into staging a 'Thriller' number for the school assembly. We went all out, with fake gravestones and costumes and everything. There were twelve of us dancing and singing—and I got to do the Michael Jackson part! Everyone loved it—and since the assembly was taped, we had an instant music video!"

In a great music video, everything comes together in an awesome way. The idea, the song, the singing, the dancing, the acting, the costumes, the setting—all of these elements work together to tell a fab story—in music!

Obviously you want your video to stand out and totally rock. To make it special, it's important for you to spend time doing some (fun!) homework before your shoot.

> "I WAS JUST POSTING VIDEOS ONLINE FOR FUN. I NEVER REALLY THOUGHT THIS [REACTION] WAS POSSIBLE, SO I NEVER REALLY DREAMED OF IT. IT'S ... JUST KIND OF SURREAL."
>
> —JUSTIN BIEBER

Do Your Homework: Watch Music Videos!

The best way to get ideas for making your own music videos is to watch lots of them. You can go to KIDZ BOP and watch tons of them! As you watch the videos, write down what videos you loved and why you loved them, as well as the ones you didn't like and why.

You may think you'll remember, but after watching twenty to thirty videos, trust us, you will forget. Taking notes also helps you pay closer attention to the smaller, less-noticeable things that add to making each video a great video, or a video bomb.

KIDZ BOP NOTES: ASK YOUR MOM FIRST

There are other places that show music videos, like YouTube, but they are not for kids. If you want to check them out, ask for your parents' permission, or better yet, ask them if they'll help you search for appropriate videos and watch with you on these sites (all of which have age requirements):

YouTube.com
Myspace.com
Reverbnation.com
Facebook.com

Five Steps to a Great Music Video

Making cool music videos is easy when you follow these five steps.

Step One: Get a Great Idea

After you have watched a lot of videos and know what you like and why, it's time to brainstorm ideas for your own video. Brainstorming means letting your brain go a bit crazy, coming up with everything from simple ideas to wacky ideas.

Dream up as many ideas as possible—and write them all down. You can also brainstorm with your parents and friends. Write down all the ideas (even if they don't sound great at the time), putting stars next to the ones that sound really good to you.

"YOU HAVE TO BELIEVE IN LOVE STORIES AND PRINCE CHARMINGS AND HAPPILY EVER AFTER. THAT'S WHY I WRITE THESE SONGS. BECAUSE I THINK LOVE IS FEARLESS."

—TAYLOR SWIFT

Ideally, you want to come up with something new, something that sets you apart from all the other KIDZ BOP Kids. You want a music video that shows you can sing and dance and act or write songs or whatever—something that shows the world who you are and why you're unique and fun and super-talented.

Step Two: Plan Your Shoot

If you're just doing something quick and easy with a Flip cam like Steffan, you may not need to plan much. Just sing and shoot!

You can always make it more interesting by shooting:

In different places—like Charisma's dad did for her "Teardrops on My Guitar" music video.

From different camera positions—like close-ups and long shots and cutaways (times when the camera is focused on your hands or your guitar or piano keys).

You doing different things—playing an instrument, dancing, etc.

Let your imagination go wild! This is the time to be really creative and let your colorful side show. Dream up interesting ways you can make your video really different and then block out different "scenes" (first you're on your bed, then you're in your yard, etc.).

If you want to make a video that's a little story, like Elijah's "Thriller" number, you'll need to give it some more thought.

Elijah already had his story—"Thriller" is a story song. All he had to do was use it—and plan the video according to the song. You can do the same thing with any story song, or you can make up your own.

A story video is like a little movie. In "Thriller," a graveyard comes to life. Just write down what happens in the song, and how you can shoot it. If you can draw, you can even draw it out like a cartoon (in what's called a storyboard).

KIDZ BOP SAYS: ASK PERMISSION

If you want to shoot your music video in a public setting (like your school or your favorite local pizza place), ask the person in charge (the principal of your school, the restaurant manager if it's a restaurant) if you can use their public location for an hour or two.

Step Three: Get Your Stuff Together

You need to get your stuff together before you shoot. Here are some of the things you might need for your music video:

Props. Ask your family and friends first, and then if you need special props, it's time to brainstorm on how to find what you need. Before paying for anything, try asking friends of friends or your teacher or your coach or local businesses to see if they—or someone they know—might have what you need.

Costumes. Costumes are fun—and can help make your video stand out. Be creative! What you wear should reveal your personality and make you and your band stand out. If you're shooting a story song like "Thriller," you may need unique costumes. Make them yourself, or ask friends and family for help. You can also try the drama club at school, or local thrift stores, flea markets, costume stores, party stores, or even theater groups. (They might have costumes they can loan you.)

People. Do you want singers, dancers, or other people for your music video? If you're with a band, you can start with your bandmates—and add people as needed. Enlist your friends and family—they'll love to help! You can also ask the kids in your drama club, dance school, etc.

Equipment. What you need could include cameras (Flip, video camera, etc.), lights, cables, extension cords, musical instruments, etc. Get your dad or favorite geek to help you with this part.

Step Four: Shoot It!

It's show time! Get everything ready. If you're not shooting at home, make sure you arrive at the site early to do this. Remember: You're the director and producer, which means it's your shoot and you have to make sure that everything goes as planned.

For extra credit: Shoot more video than you'll need. Then, you'll be able to pick and choose what goes in the final video from everything you shot.

Step Five: Edit It!

If you're shooting a performance straight through without any special effects, you may be able to skip this step. But if you're into editing video or you know someone else who is—like your dad—you can edit your music video into something really special. Have fun with it!

KIDZ BOP Notes: Throw a Premiere Party!

When your music video is ready, post it on KIDZ BOP and ask your parents if you can celebrate its premiere with a party! Invite everyone who helped you, along with friends and family.

Whether you have a party or not, be sure to thank everyone who helps you with your music video. You can give them copies of the video when it's completed—or thank them with a homemade cake or cupcakes or cookies. Sending handwritten thank-you notes is also a very nice thing to do.

Make Your Own KIDZ BOP Webshow

Another way to showcase your talent and make new friends and fans is by creating your own webshow for KIDZBOP.com.

Webshows are cool because they can be about most anything you like. You can sing, dance, act, perform magic tricks—entertain in any way.

Or you can shoot a webshow about anything you're interested in—from your cat to horseback riding to making costumes and applying makeup. You are limited only by your imagination!

Check out KIDZBOP.com to see all the webshows other kids have made and posted—and then get started on your own!

How to Talk to Your Fans

The only thing more exciting than having fans is actually interacting with them! It's easy to do online at KIDZBOP.com. All you need to do is update your status using SafeText. You'll love talking to your fans—but do be careful. Don't give out too much personal information about yourself. Better safe than sorry!

Book Your First Play Dates!

Making music videos is fun, but there's nothing like performing for a live audience. Now that you're ready to wow 'em, take your show on the road.

You can start in your own backyard. You can perform for friends' parties, your school, your church, local fairs and farmer's markets, and your local community center. You can compete in talent shows, audition for local theatrical productions, sign up for fundraisers or town assemblies—any event where entertainers perform.

Use your imagination—and start booking gigs! But do keep in mind that people just starting out in music mostly perform for free. In the beginning, most singers and dancers are happy just to be seen. Performing anywhere helps you become much better, so it "pays off" in ways that don't involve money.

When You Play

Before you perform, get ready. Line up everything and everyone you'll need to set up and play. Make sure your bandmates and/or helpers can do whatever it is you need them to do. Here's a to-do list:

★ Line up your equipment. Make sure you have all the cords and stuff that you'll need.

★ Make your set list of songs you'll play and in what order you'll play them.

★ Practice, practice, practice for at least five days leading up to the event and most particularly on the night before—but don't strain your voice!

★ Think about what you'll say between songs.

★ Remember to thank everyone.

★ Pack up your equipment and leave the performance area clean and organized.

★ Call the next day to thank the person who booked you. Ask if they have another day open for you to play.

Make Your Own CDs

When you have at least three songs you perform well, think about making your own CD. Sure, the big stars record their songs at a recording studio, but you can do it right at home. Just ask your dad or your favorite geek to do it for you. They'll know what to do—and how to do it.

If you're a singer/songwriter, make sure you pick three songs that show off your songwriting skills (lyrics especially), your ability to play a guitar (or a keyboard or a piano, etc.), and your voice. If you're a singer, choose songs that show off your voice, your vocal range, and how well you sing other people's songs. If you're a band, you want to rock it on all counts.

Once you've got your CDs, you can sell them to your fans after your performances.

Band on the Run

> "GETTING TO TRAVEL THE WORLD AND PLAY MY SONGS HAS TO BE ONE OF THE BEST JOBS IN THE WORLD."
>
> —COLBIE CAILLAT

Touring is every performer's dream. Playing all the big cities around the globe—from New York City and San Francisco to London and Paris and back again—is exciting. Who wouldn't want to perform in front of screaming fans the world over?

You may dream of the day you hit the road as a performer—and may your dreams come true!—but life on tour is a little more complicated. Let's take a look at the pros and cons—and pros again—of the concert circuit.

The Truth about Touring

It may sound glamorous—and it is! But going on tour is also hard work. Long hours on the road, performing every day, a blur of new places and people—it's a full-time job!

And unless it's summer, you'll also have to keep up with your school work. It's not only good for you to get an education, it's the law. Some kids only tour during the summer and vacations, so they can go to school at home the rest of the year. Other kids, like Taylor Swift, are home-schooled. If you'd rather be on the road, then make the time to study, and keep your grades up.

What you decide to do will depend upon the nature of the opportunities that present themselves, your personal and professional preferences, and how your parents feel about it.

Speaking of parents. . . .

How to Keep Your Parents from Freaking Out

The easiest way to keep your parents from freaking out as your career takes off is to take them with you. Pull a Justin Bieber or a Miley Cyrus, and invite your folks on the road with you. You need grownups you can trust to travel with you—why not the adults you can trust the most? Nobody cares more about you than your parents, so think about it:

★ Your mom can be your "momager"—and make sure that you eat right, get enough sleep, and squeeze in some downtime so that you don't wear yourself out.

★ Your dad can be your "dadager"—and book your shows for you.

★ Your sister can be your roadie, your brother can make your banners, your aunt can handle your merchandise.

You're going to need your parents' permission anyway—and this may help you get it!

So hit the road with your family, and give the people what they want: you, onstage, performing for them. This is what being an entertainer is all about. So enjoy it—and go for broke!

Welcome to KIDZ BOP Pop Stardom!

Congratulations, you're on your way! You've mastered the art of performing—and are coming into your own as an entertainer. Life is about to speed up, big time, as you rocket into stardom!

It's official! You're a KIDZ BOP Pop Star now.

Get ready to rock! And remember: We want to hear all about it. So keep in touch and let us know at KIDZBOP.com how you're doing, and how we can help you make all of your showbiz dreams come true.

And now, the show must go on! Your audience is waiting. . . . Break a leg!

STEFFAN: "Being a KIDZ BOP Kid is great—but I didn't want it to freak out my friends back home. Like I was conceited now or something. So I don't make a big deal out of it—and count on them to make sure I don't get a big head."

HANNA: "The hardest part is balancing school and show business. It's a lot of work—but it's definitely worth it!"

EVA: "Don't let haters get you down. They're just jealous—because they're not you! That's what my mom told me when some mean girls at school made fun of my singing—and she was right. But now that I'm a KIDZ BOP Kid, they all want to be my friend!"

CHARISMA: "Always remember to be sweet to your fans. I go out of my way to be nice to them, because I know they love me and helped me to get where I am today—and where I'm going tomorrow!"

ELIJAH: "I love being a KIDZ BOP Kid! I work hard—but I love every minute! Take it from me—it just doesn't get any better than this. So enjoy yourself—because you are on your way!"

INDEX

Get an awesome
FREE KIDZ BOP song!

JUST FOLLOW THESE SIMPLE STEPS:

1. Go to *www.KIDZBOP.com/KidzBopBooks*
2. Enter your 10-digit code
3. Click "Submit"
4. Choose the KIDZ BOP song you'd like to download
5. Once your FREE KIDZ BOP download is complete, rock out!